Breaking the Chains
That **Anchors**

Shanique Bruce

Copyright ©2024 Shanique Bruce

ISBN: 978-1-954755-43-7

All rights reserved. No part of this publication may be reproduced, copied, stored in a retrieval system, transmitted, or scanned in any form or under any conditions, including, photocopying, electronic, recording, or otherwise, without the written permission of the author, Shanique Bruce.

Published and formatted by:
Restoration of the Breach Without Borders
West Palm Beach
Fl, 33407

Cover design by:
Leostone Morrison

Contents

Dedication	iv
Acknowledgment	vi
Foreword	viii
Introduction	xi
Chapter 1: Confronting the Weight of Attachment	1
Chapter 2: Anchored in Yesteryear	15
Chapter 3: The Pull of Nostalgia	26
Chapter 4: Unraveling the Threads of the Past	36
Chapter 5: Forgiveness	57
Chapter 6: Let It Go	70
Chapter 7: Breaking out of Limiting Beliefs	82
Chapter 8: Stay Teachable	93
Chapter 9: Take Responsibility	103
Chapter 10: Embracing the Growth Mindset	111
Chapter 11: Embracing the Unknown	127
Chapter 12: Rewriting The Narrative	144
Conclusion	157
Salvation Prayer	162
About the Author	164

Dedication

To my extraordinary mother, Suzette Findlay, whose unwavering strength and resilience inspire me daily. Despite her past challenges, she has emerged as a symbol of hope, like a Phoenix rising from the ashes. Thank you for showing me what it means to leave behind the places we've outgrown and embrace the transformative power of change.

To my loving husband, Jahmoy Bruce, your constant support and belief in me have been the anchor that grounds me during times of uncertainty. Your presence and love have given me the courage and strength to step into the unknown and embrace new beginnings.

To my daughter, Paige-Amoy, and my brother, Delany, you are the driving force behind every decision I make. May all documented in this book serve as a reminder that you also have the power to leave behind what no longer serves you and embrace a life of authenticity and fulfillment.

Acknowledgment

I would like to express my deepest gratitude to The Most High God, who came and died to grant us liberation from whatever holds us captive. His love and grace have been my constant source of strength throughout this writing process.

I am incredibly thankful to the Holy Spirit for the inspiration and guidance that came through His subtle voice, leading me on the path illuminated by His wisdom. It is through His gentle nudges, whispering, "This is the way, walk in it," that I found the courage to embrace change and leave behind the places I've outgrown.

I extend my heartfelt appreciation to Alicia Gow, Donna Morris, and Rev. Leostone Morrison for their invaluable insights and encouragement. They helped me realize the power of changing my mindset and seeing the world through the lens of God's vision. This new mindset has catapulted me from the past and has led me to leave behind the things, people, and places that no longer serve me.

Finally, I want to express my gratitude to my readers, who will embark on this journey of embracing change and leaving behind what no longer serves them. Your willingness to explore these pages is a testament to your courage and desire for personal growth. Thank you for joining me on this transformative journey.

Foreword

I am honored to write this foreword for Shanique Bruce's transformative book, *"Anchored in the Past: Breaking the Chains That Anchors"*. Shanique, a dear friend and fellow laborer in the Kingdom, has done an outstanding job with this work. First and foremost, I want to thank the Holy Spirit for birthing this book, as it is truly a divine download from heaven.

'Anchored in the Past' offers transformative insights that empower readers to break free from the chains of their past and embrace change. Shanique highlights the truth that we don't have to let life pass us by—we can be active participants in the transformation we desire. Through Christ, we can do all things, as Philippians 4:13 reminds us: *"I can do all things through Christ who strengthens me."*

The anchors in life, though often weighing us down, do not have to hold us back. By stepping out in faith and being intentional about your mindset, you can break free from the past. As you explore the message of this book, be assured that you have the power to choose not to remain anchored in yesterday's struggles. God wants to set you free today!

With this book in your hands, you will learn how to release the weight of unforgiveness and discover how letting go can unlock new beginnings. Embracing a forgiving spirit allows God's perfect plan to unfold in your life.

I commend the author for writing such a compelling and timely book. Her testimonies have brought much encouragement. It's a true guide for anyone ready to embrace change and leave behind the places they have outgrown. While the unknown may be intimidating, it is precisely where the potential for growth and transformation lies. Now is the time to let go of the comfort zone mindset and be truly anchored in the present.

This book is a must-have and a must-read. It is packed with scripture to guide you on your journey of forgiveness, and it overflows with divine knowledge and wisdom. As you dive into its pages, you will cultivate a growth mindset that empowers you to step out of every narrative that keeps you anchored in the past.

Be richly blessed, and don't hesitate to share this book with your family and friends, so that others can experience the same.

-Min Donna Morris
Author, Speaker, Mentor, Coach
"Moved to a New Mindset, Free from limitations rejections, and fears".

Introduction

Are you anchored in the past? Are you able to recognize if you are anchored?

In life's journey, we often find ourselves bound by the chains of the past. Memories, experiences, and attachments can entangle us, hindering our growth and preventing us from reaching our true potential. But what if we could break free from these binds and embrace the transformative power of change?

Change is an inevitable part of life yet letting go of the places we've outgrown can be exceptionally challenging. In *"Anchored in the Past,"* we embark on a journey of exploring the profound struggles and emotions associated with leaving familiar territories. This book delves into the reasons why detachment from our roots is so difficult, examines the impact of staying in stagnant environments, and offers insightful strategies to cope with the transformative process.

Throughout this book, we'll draw inspiration from real-life stories, existing research, and the timeless wisdom of biblical narratives. By exploring the experiences of iconic biblical heroes who contended with the pull of the past, the weight of attachment, and the courage required to forge a new path, we'll uncover profound lessons that can guide us on our journeys of personal and spiritual transformation.

Through this process of deep introspection, we'll work to break free from the limiting beliefs and self-imposed constraints that have prevented us from reaching our fullest potential. Whether it's the societal conditioning that has shaped our values and priorities, or the personal traumas and disappointments that have left an unforgettable mark on our psyche, this book will empower us to rewrite the narrative and forge a new path forward.

As we shed the weight of the past, we'll find ourselves standing at the edge of the unknown, faced with the exhilarating prospect of embracing change and reinventing ourselves. This journey will not be easy – change rarely is – but the rewards that await us on the other side are immeasurable. By letting go of the familiar and the comfortable, we open ourselves up to a world of possibility, one where we can truly live in alignment with our deepest values and highest aspirations.

Through personal growth, cultural references, philosophical analysis, and biblical references, *"Anchored in the Past"* invites readers to embark on a transformative journey. From the pull of nostalgia to the liberation of breaking free, this book will serve as a roadmap for those seeking to cultivate the courage, resilience, and vision required to navigate the uncharted waters of the present and the future.

This book offers a roadmap to navigate the difficulties of change. It reveals the strength hidden within, the resilience required to face the unknown, and the profound wisdom that comes from stepping into unfamiliar territory. Let these pages guide you towards breaking free from the shackles of the past and discovering the exhilarating freedom that accompanies embracing change. Your journey toward self-discovery and personal fulfillment starts here.

So, let us begin this journey together, ready to confront the weight of our attachments, unravel the constraints of the past, and emerge, reborn, into a life of greater authenticity, fulfillment, and purpose. The path ahead may be uncertain, but it is also brimming with possibility – if only we dare to take the first step, guided by the timeless wisdom of those who have walked this road before us.

Chapter 1
Confronting the weight of Attachment

"What if she never spoke to me again? What if I was labeled as ingrate or worse, a user"?

As human beings, we have an innate tendency to cling to the familiar - the people, the things, the environments, and the situations that have become interwoven into the fabric of our lives. This attachment, born out of a deep-seated desire for security and belonging, can often become a heavy burden that we carry, unaware of how it is stunting our growth and preventing us from embracing the necessary changes that life presents.

In the book of Genesis, we see a poignant example of the weight of attachment in the story of Abraham, Hagar, and their son, Ishmael. Abraham, bound by his love for his firstborn son, struggled to let go of the attachment he had formed, even when God called him to a new path. Hagar, too, clung to the only life she had known, unable to see beyond the confines of her circumstances.

It is a tale that echoes the experiences of many of us, as we find ourselves clinging to relationships, possessions, or situations that no longer serve us, simply because the thought of letting go is too painful to bear. We fear the unknown, the uncertainty that lies beyond the familiar, and so we choose to remain tethered to the anchors of our past, even as they weigh us down.

There was a time in my life when I found myself clinging to a relationship that no longer served me. It was a friendship that had once been a beacon of light, a source of comfort and support during one of my darkest periods.

But as the years passed, the dynamic had shifted, morphing into something altogether more toxic and taxing, to say the least.

Looking back, I can see now how the pull of nostalgia and my deep-seated need for that connection kept me tethered to this person, even as the relationship became increasingly draining and unhealthy. She had been there for me when I needed her most, and the thought of severing that bond filled me with a profound sense of guilt and unease.

After all, I was supposed to be the grateful one, the friend who remained loyal and steadfast no matter the circumstances. The idea of confronting the toxicity, of acknowledging that this relationship was no longer working for me, filled me with a deep sense of dread.

What if she never spoke to me again? What if I was labeled as ungrateful or even worse, a user?

As a chronic people-pleaser, the thought of rocking the boat, of prioritizing my own needs over hers, was utterly terrifying. I had spent so much time and energy trying to be the perfect friend, the one who never disappointed or let anyone down. And now, here I was, faced with the prospect of doing the very thing she had always inspired me to do - speak my truth.

But the weight of that attachment, the emotional baggage that came with it, had become too much to bear. The constant drama, the passive-aggressive jabs, the ever-shifting power dynamics - it was all-consuming, draining the very life out of me. I knew, deep down, that this relationship was no longer serving me, and that it was time to let go.

Yet, the decision to do so was agonizingly difficult. I replayed scenarios in my mind, imagining the hurt and betrayal in her eyes, the accusations of selfishness and ingratitude. The fear of losing her, of severing that vital connection, loomed large, paralyzing me with indecision.

It was in those moments of turmoil that I had to confront the harsh reality - the person I once knew and cherished was no longer the same. The friendship had become toxic and my continued presence in it was only perpetuating the cycle of hurt and resentment.

As I wrestled with this realization, I found myself at a crossroads. I could either continue to cling to the remnants of what once was, or I could muster the courage to let go and embrace the unknown. It was a decision that weighed heavily on my heart, but ultimately, I knew that my well-being had to take priority.

With a trembling hand, I reached out, voicing my concerns, my needs, and my truth. The conversation was painful and emotional, and the outcome was uncertain. But at that moment, I chose to honour myself, to break free from the chains of attachment that had been holding me back.

It was a decision that came at a great cost - the loss of a friendship that had once been so integral to my life. But as I navigated the aftermath, I found peace in the knowledge that I had done the difficult, yet necessary, thing. I had chosen to confront the weight of my attachment, to let go of what no longer served me, and to embrace the possibility of a future unchained to the past.

The future was undefined, but I no longer feared it. I had taken the first step towards reclaiming my identity and towards living a life that was truly my own. And in that, I found a profound sense of liberation - a freedom that was worth the pain of confronting the weight of my attachment.

And it is not just our attachments that can hold us back. Sometimes, those closest to us, the very people who have been our pillars of support, can become obstacles to our progress. They, too, can become so deeply invested in the roles we play in their lives that they are unwilling to let us go, even when our growth demands it. We have to stretch beyond our relationships and environment.

One of my favourite bible characters taught me a very important lesson about not being limited to the confines of our environment. Peter, in Matthew chapter fourteen taught me that when we go beyond our environment, we may sink but we can create history. Peter was in the boat, his environment, though the waves were crashing against the boat he was in his safe place.

He was a fisherman, He had most likely experienced storms before so of course, he knew what to do. What he had never experienced before was a ghost, so He began to scream with the others who were in the boat "Ghost!" but Jesus, made known himself to them and Peter was willing to stretch, willing to confront the weight of attachment, said: *"If it is you, call me to come"* and with the word that went forth from Jesus' mouth Peter climbed out of the boat and began walking on water. Surely, he took his eyes off the master, and he sank but Peter is the only human other than Jesus that is recorded to have ever walked on water. He made history because he didn't stay in his safe place.

God will uphold you just like he upheld Peter, you cannot sink, and if you feel like you are sinking, cry out to Jesus.

What do you need to achieve that has never been done in your family? What do you need to do that will push you? What has God told you to do?

God called Abraham, out from among his family, his safe place. One of the key lessons we can learn from Abraham's journey is the importance of -confronting the weight of attachment. By leaving his home and family behind, Abraham was forced to confront his attachment to the things and people he had known his entire life. This was not an easy process, but it was a necessary one if he was to fulfill his destiny.

The story of Abraham begins with him living a comfortable life in the city of Ur, surrounded by his family and possessions. But God calls him to leave everything behind and journey to a land that he has never seen before. As the Bible recounts, *"The Lord had said to Abram, 'Go from your country, your people, and your father's household to the land I will show you.'"* (Genesis 12:1)

This command must have been incredibly difficult for Abraham to accept. After all, he had built a life in Ur – a life that he was familiar with and comfortable in. He had his home, his family, and his belongings. Leaving all of that behind and venturing into the unknown must have been a terrifying demand on him.

Yet, despite his attachments, Abraham ultimately chose to obey God's call. He gathered his wife, Sarai, and his nephew, Lot, and set out on a journey to an unknown destination. This act of faith and trust in God's plan was a profound demonstration of Abraham's willingness to let go of the familiar and embrace the unknown.

As Abraham journeyed, he encountered many challenges and obstacles. The road was long and demanding, and he had to navigate unfamiliar terrain and cultures. At times, he must have longed for the comforts of his old life in Ur. But through it all, he remained steadfast in his commitment to God's plan for his life.

Ultimately, the story of Abraham's journey serves as a powerful reminder that confronting our attachments and embracing the unknown can be a transformative and rewarding experience. By letting go of the familiar and embracing the unknown, we can not only improve our lives but also contribute to the greater good. No athlete wins without doing uncomfortable things. When you are in a zone you may believe that's the best you can be, so you have to stretch.

In these instances, the weight of attachment can become a heavy burden, as we find ourselves torn between the needs of our loved ones and the call of our truth. We can become paralyzed, unwilling to take the leap of faith that could lead us to a brighter future, for fear of losing the connections that have sustained us.

But the reality is, that true growth and transformation often require us to confront the weight of attachment head-on. It is only by acknowledging the hold that these connections have on us, and making the courageous decision to let go, that we can truly step into the fullness of who we are meant to become.

As we navigate this journey, it is important to remember that the brain, wired for survival, often interprets change and loss as a threat, triggering a powerful emotional response that can make it feel impossible to let go. The fear of the unknown, the grief over what we are leaving behind, and the uncertainty of the future can all converge, creating a formidable obstacle to our growth.

But with self-awareness, compassion, and a willingness to confront the weight of attachment, we can learn to navigate these challenges with grace and resilience. We can acknowledge the depth of our feelings, while also recognizing that the path forward may require us to make difficult choices that prioritize our own well-being and personal growth.

As we embark on this journey, let us remember the words of the Psalmist: *"The Lord is my strength and my shield; my heart trusts in him, and he helps me"* (Psalm 28:7).

With God's guidance and the support of our community, we can find the courage to let go of the things that no longer serve us, and embrace the new horizons that await

How can I Confront the Weight of Attachment?

Practice self-awareness by regularly reflecting on the attachments in your life and how they are impacting your growth and well-being. Always be willing to cultivate self-compassion in understanding that the desire to cling to the familiar is a deeply human experience, and approach yourself with kindness as you navigate this challenge.

Surround yourself with a community of loved ones who can offer encouragement, wisdom, and accountability as you confront the weight of attachment. Never fail to embrace the unknown. Remind yourself that the unknown, while scary, is also full of possibility. Lean into the uncertainty with an open and curious mindset.

Prioritize your well-being, remembering that your growth and personal development should be the primary focus. And be willing to make the difficult choices that prioritize your own needs and long-term fulfillment. Trust in the divine by leaning on your faith, and trust that God is guiding you through this process, even when the path ahead is unclear. Seek His wisdom and strength to navigate the weight of attachment.

Letting go is not might not be easy. It requires courage, vulnerability, and a willingness to sit with the discomfort of the unfamiliar. It means acknowledging that the very things we have cherished may no longer be serving us and having the strength to release our grasp. This process can be messy and painful, as we grieve the loss of what once was. But on the other side lies the freedom to create a new path, to shape our lives according to our highest aspirations rather than our past limitations.

Chapter 2
Anchored in Yesteryear

Are You Anchored to Yesteryear?

They fell deeply in love and Joy thought she had found her happy ever after. When they first met years ago, John was the charming, attentive partner she had always dreamed of. Now she finds herself trapped in an abusive relationship. Over time, his behaviour began to change. He would become angry and volatile, particularly after he had been drinking. The verbal abuse soon escalated into physical violence, with John lashing out and hitting her. She had often suggested that they go to counselling to address the challenges in their marriage and that he get the help, he needed regarding his alcoholism; however, he would quickly dismiss her suggestions. Yet, despite the pain and fear, Joy found herself clinging to the memories of the man she had fallen in love with - she was sure that the man she married was still in there, waiting to resurface.

"He promised he would change," Joy would tell herself, holding onto the hope that the loving, gentle John would return.

"If I try harder and do everything right, maybe he'll stop hitting me. I believe the man I married is still in there.

Tragically, Joy's story is not uncommon. Studies show that the average woman in an abusive relationship will attempt to leave seven times before she is finally able to break free. Many stay, convinced that their partner will reform, and the relationship will return to the way it once was - a phenomenon known as "anchoring to yesteryear."

This psychological phenomenon occurs when individuals become fixated on the past, unable to let go of the idealized version of a person or situation. They cling to the memories of how things used to be, refusing to accept the harsh reality of the present. In the case of an abusive relationship, the victim may hold onto the belief that their partner will change, even in the face of mounting evidence to the contrary.

It is my sincere prayer, that all of us can one day like Paul say in Philippians 3:13,

> *"But one thing I do: Forgetting what is behind and straining toward what is ahead."*

Yet for those trapped in abusive situations, the pull of the past can be incredibly strong, leaving them feeling paralyzed and unable to move forward. The consequences of remaining anchored to yesteryear can be devastating. Studies have shown that victims of domestic abuse who stay in their relationships are at a much higher risk of severe injury or even death.

The psychological toll is also immense, with victims often experiencing long-lasting trauma, depression, and anxiety.

I understand that when the circumstances of our lives are less than ideal; often, it's not that we don't want to make a change, but rather that we're paralyzed by the fear of the unknown. The thought of starting over, of venturing into uncharted territory, can be very unsettling.

At the heart of this hesitation is a fundamental human need for stability and predictability. We crave the comfort of the known, the security of the familiar, because it offers a sense of control and certainty in an unpredictable world. After all, if we've already experienced something, we at least know what to expect – or so we think.

This mindset can be a powerful trap, keeping us connected to situations or relationships that no longer serve us. We may find ourselves stuck in unfulfilling jobs, unhealthy habits, or dysfunctional situations, all because the prospect of starting anew is simply too overwhelming.

If this describes your situation, it may be time for you to seek assistance. It is not enough for us to sit and endure these difficult moments hoping the other party or situation will change. Seeking spiritual intervention is important, God can turn anything around, however, what do you do in the waiting period? It is not enough to sit in any situation that no longer serves you because you are waiting for the change to come. Take steps to facilitate the change you want to see.

Many of us say, well that's not my situation. I am not being abused physically, but are you enduring hardship in any way, shape, or form, and are you living in yesterday's memories? Are you holding on to something that you know no longer serves you?

We may stay in a job that drains our energy and creativity, simply because it's a known quantity. The prospect of searching for a new position, navigating the interview process, and potentially facing uncertainty, can feel like an insurmountable challenge. We convince ourselves that the devil we know is better than the one we don't.

But the truth is, the unknown, while overwhelming, also holds the potential for growth, fulfillment, and ultimately, a more authentic and satisfying life. By stepping out of our comfort zones and embracing the uncertainties of the future, we open ourselves up to new experiences, relationships, and opportunities that can enrich our lives in ways we never imagined.

It's important to recognize that the fear of starting over is a natural human response, rooted in our natural desire for security and familiarity. However, we need to challenge this fear and cultivate the courage to take calculated risks and step into the unknown.

This may involve small, gradual steps – trying a new hobby, reaching out to a potential new friend, or exploring a different career path. Each step, no matter how seemingly insignificant, can help build the confidence and resilience needed to tackle larger, more daunting challenges.

Ultimately, the choice to leave the familiar behind and start over is a deeply personal one, but it's a decision that can lead to profound personal growth, self-discovery, and a deeper sense of fulfillment. We may just find that the most rewarding experiences lie beyond the boundaries of the familiar and embrace the unknown.

As we see in the story of Lot's wife, being *"anchored to yesteryear"* can have devastating consequences. When God called Lot and his family to flee the doomed city of Sodom, Lot's wife, unable to let go of the life she had known, looked back and was turned into a pillar of salt. This powerful story serves as a warning- those who are unwilling to let go of the past, risk becoming frozen in time, unable to move forward.

God's desire for us is not to be shackled to the past, but to be liberated by the future. Through the sacrifice of Jesus Christ, we have been allowed to break free from the chains that have held us captive. We are no longer bound by the mistakes or tragedies of our yesteryear but empowered to embrace the new life that God has in store for us.

Joy eventually summoned the courage to seek help and walked away from the abusive relationship that had consumed her for so long. She recognized that the man she married was gone and that the only way forward was to let go of the past and embrace the future free of violence and fear.

Will it be easy, no! Most of us have experienced a breakup or two in our lifetime, some after dating for a short time while others may experience this after dating for years. The time invested didn't take away from the fact that we had just experienced a loss, so we sat and cried for days, weeks, or even months. Looking back, we know it was a decision we had to make, I am sure we can now see why severing those ties was important. It won't be easy, but with the steadfast love and guidance of God, just like Joy, we can find the strength to break free from the anchor of yesteryear.

The good news is, that through the authority that we have obtained from Christ Jesus, breaking free from the anchor of the past is possible. It requires a willingness to honestly assess the current situation, to let go of the idealized version of the person or relationship, and to take decisive action toward a better future.

This may involve seeking professional counseling, reaching out to support networks, or even making the difficult decision to leave the relationships that no longer serve us be it platonic or otherwise.

Quiz

Are you anchored in Yesteryear? Take this quiz and see what your scores imply.

1. Do you find yourself constantly reminiscing about the "good old days"?

    o Yes

    o No

2. Do you keep significant mementos, photos, or objects from your past that you find hard to get rid of?

    o Yes

    o No

3. When faced with change or new experiences, do you often feel anxious or resistant?

    o Yes

    o No

4. Do you feel a strong attachment to your childhood home or the places you grew up?

    o Yes

    o No

5. Do you find yourself often wishing you could go back in time to relive certain moments from your past?

    o   Yes
    o   No

Scoring:

If you answered **"Yes"** to **4 or more** of these questions, you may be struggling to let go of the past and move forward.

Chapter 3
The Pull of Nostalgia

I understood their reasoning - they wanted me to spread my wings, step out into the world, and become the independent young woman they knew I could be. Yet, the prospect of leaving the only true home I had known for the past eight years filled me with a profound sense of fear and anxiety.

When I was 18 years old, I had made the difficult decision to drop out of university, my dreams of higher education were cut short by a lack of funds. I had moved to another parish to pursue higher education and within a year, I decided to go back home to my adopted family, the pillars of stability in my life, they welcomed me back into their home with open arms. There, within those four walls, I had found consolation, I began rebuilding the shattered pieces of my confidence and rediscovering my sense of purpose.

Within six months of coming back home, that sense of security quickly came to an end. My adopted parents, in a decision that I knew, came from a place of love, had decided that it was time for me to move out on my own. Just as an eagle stirs its nest, forcing its young to take flight, they were gently but firmly pushing me out of the comfortable confines of this space, compelling me to forge a new path.

I had grown so accustomed to the safety and familiarity of my room, of that house, that the thought of venturing out into the unknown was both exhilarating and terrifying.

I can still remember when I moved out and moved into my first apartment. I remember how the weight of my decision settled heavily upon my shoulders. The familiar surroundings of my adopted parents' home had been a comfort, a refuge from the storms of the past year. It was a sanctuary where I knew what to expect, where the very walls seemed to whisper reassurances of safety and stability.

I remember gazing around the room and couldn't help but feel a sense of longing for that comforting familiarity. The brain, wired to seek out that which is known and predictable, naturally pulled me back toward the past, offering the seductive embrace of nostalgia. It was a siren's call, luring me with the false promise of security - like the Israelites in the wilderness, who had longed to return to the perceived safety of Egypt, conveniently forgetting the harsh realities of their bondage.

"If only we had died by the Lord's hand in Egypt!" They had cried, "At least there we had food to eat." (Exodus 16:3)

Their fear was whitewashed by the pull of the familiar. In their fear of the unknown, they had failed to see the true liberation that awaited them, the boundless provision and protection of a God who had promised to be their steady guide.

And so, it is with us, when faced with the scary decision of leaving behind the familiar, even if it no longer serves us. The brain, hardwired for survival, clings to the known, regardless of how limiting or even harmful it may be. The children of Israel had endured abuse and worked under harsh conditions, but it wasn't always that way and we often reflect on the positives failing to realize that the positives we experienced were in our yesterday. For those who have endured the ravages of abuse or victimization, the pull of nostalgia can be even more powerful, as the mind is on a desperate mission to return to the *"safety"* of the known, even if that safety is an illusion.

As I stood there, my gaze sweeping the bare apartment, I knew that I could not allow my fear of the unknown to anchor me to the past. That was my chance to forge a new path, to create a life that was truly my own. And while the prospect was scary, I felt a glimmer of hope kindling within me - a hope that was rooted in the promises of a God who had never abandoned me, even in the darkest of times.

"Fear not, for I am with you; be not dismayed, for I am your God. I will strengthen you, yes, I will help you, I will uphold you with My righteous right hand." (Isaiah 41:10) These were the words that echoed in my heart, a constant reminder that I was not alone, that the God who had brought me through the trials of the past year would continue to be my steady guide, even as I navigated the unfamiliar waters of this new chapter.

On your journey of embracing change and leaving behind the places that no longer serve you, the pull of nostalgia will linger, tugging at the edges of your consciousness; you cannot allow it to hold you back. For God has promised to be your constant companion, to strengthen you, and to uphold you, even amid the unknown. With His guiding hand, you can face the challenges that lie ahead, confident in the knowledge that you are never truly alone.

That period of my life was very lonely, I lacked earthly support, but I realized that there was an even greater presence that would never abandon me. As the Psalmist so beautifully wrote, *"Where can I go from Your Spirit? Or where can I flee from Your presence?"* (Psalm 139:7). No matter how far I ventured or how uncertain the path ahead, I could take comfort in the knowledge that the God who had carried me this far would never leave my side.

The avenue of change can be quite lonely, sometimes you may have to do it yourself. The friend that you go to parties with may not accompany you, and your parents may not walk the road with you, but you have to press towards the mark remembering why you started in the first place. You must keep at the forefront of your mind that your tomorrow will be greater. Never forget your why and the reward that lies ahead.

Your brain will try to comfort you with the illusions of safety and security. Every step you take your brain is equipped for existence will present arguments as to why you should take a step back but why not take another step forward?

Lisa Nichols said, *"In the pursuit of not falling, we never fly"*. Too often we reflect on the negative, what if you fall, and so what if you fall? The fall is not what is important it is what happens after you fall. What matters is what you do after you go down, what matters is what have you learned because of that fall. It is better to take a chance on you and not get the results you were working for than not to have tried and sit in regret wondering what would have happened had I ventured out.

So, as you face the decisions and transitions that lie before you, remember that you too are not alone. Whatever illusion or false comfort you may have been clinging to, know that there is a love greater than anything this world can offer. **El ROI**, The God who sees you, who knows the depths of your heart, is beckoning you to step out in faith, to let go of the anchors that are holding you back.

I encourage you to take that leap, to trust in the One who has a plan and a purpose for your life. Talk to Him, pour out your fears and your doubts, and ask for guidance to break free from the chains of the past.

In this dispensation we live in information is readily available at our fingertips, you are no longer limited poverty by or the illusion thereof. Find people who are at the place where you are trying to go. It is more challenging if you are the first in your family to do certain things or to venture out on this kind of journey, but it can be done. If you do not have examples around you, read books of people who have done it, and listen to their interviews or presentations. Do the work and be intentional in your efforts. You can choose to be an active participant in the change you want to see or you can choose to sit by waiting and hoping God will miraculously change your story without you lifting a finger. Whichever is the option you pursue, please be conscious that time is passing by. The clock is ticking, and the years are passing by hour after hour, month after month. Don't be like those who wake up and realize that twenty years have passed by and all they have acquired are accolades of excuses.

Never let this truth escape you, *"you can do all things through Christ that strengthens you"*. Therefore, stretch yourself and don't let life pass you by only reflecting on the good that you experienced in yesteryears. Your tomorrow starts today.

My friend, take heart in the knowledge that you are never alone. The God of the universe, the One who knit you together in your mother's womb, is with you every step of the way. Let go of the anchors that have been weighing you down, and step out in faith, knowing that He will guide you and sustain you, now and forevermore.

ANCHORED IN THE PAST

The pull of nostalgia can be strong, but holding on to it too tightly can prevent you from embracing the present and the future. Consider examining which aspects of the past are serving you versus holding you back, and work on finding a healthy balance between honouring your history and living fully in the now.

You seem able to appreciate your history while also being open to new experiences and growth. Keep up the great work in maintaining that forward-looking perspective!

Chapter 4
Unraveling the Threads of the Past

Many moons ago when I learnt embroidery, we would carefully create these beautiful intricate designs and then begin to bring these designs to life by using our hands to create our magic with needle and thread, not those fancy sewing machines they now have. We would spend hours on these designs and funny enough when we were close to finishing, we would often notice a mistake in our work. To fix it, we would have to patiently undo the stitches, thread by thread, to correct the error and preserve the wholeness of the design. Similarly, we sometimes need to step back and thoughtfully untangle the deeply intertwined strands that make up our identity.

Letting go of the past and the things that no longer serve us can be a profoundly challenging, yet necessary, part of our personal growth and transformation. Our lives are like a finely manufactured material, made up of many delicate threads woven together. Our experiences, relationships, and choices have created this intricate design. At times, we may need to carefully unravel the threads that have become tightly woven into our identity and sense of self. It's a complex process, like undoing the detailed embroidery of a beautiful artwork - it takes patience, care, and a willingness to address any problems we find.

The process of unravelling the past is multi-faceted, requiring both courage and compassion. Psychologically, it involves a deep dive into our subconscious, unearthing the beliefs, experiences, and attachments that have been shaping our thoughts, emotions, and behaviours, often without our conscious awareness.

Unravelling the threads of the past can be a deeply challenging and uncomfortable process, but it is often a necessary step in moving forward and finding healing. Revisiting painful memories and confronting our failures can be excruciating, as it forces us to confront the darkest moments of our lives. However, it is in these moments of vulnerability and honesty that we can find the light to guide us towards a brighter future.

When we find ourselves facing the shadows of our past, it is natural to feel a sense of disappointment. We may want to avoid the discomfort and the feelings of shame, guilt, or regret that come with revisiting these experiences. However, it is in these moments that we are called to have the courage to face our skeletons head-on.

I had to revisit the painful moment of dropping out of university in order to plan adequately when I reapplied. Many of us have similar stories that have left deep scars on our hearts and minds. We may have experienced failures, disappointments, or traumas that have shaken the very foundations of our lives. In these moments, it can feel as if we are standing amid a vast, dark abyss, with no hope of ever finding our way out.

But it is in these moments, that we must remember to pray that the power of the light of Jesus will illuminate our situation. Just as God looked upon the darkness and proclaimed, "Let there be light," we too can call upon the divine light to guide us through the shadows.

The process of unraveling the threads of the past is not an easy one, but it is a necessary part of the journey towards healing and growth. As we confront our failures and the wounds of our past, we are allowed to see ourselves and our lives from a new perspective. We can begin to understand the lessons that these experiences have taught us, and how they have shaped us into the individuals we are today.

One of the key aspects of this process is the willingness to be vulnerable and honest with ourselves.

It takes immense courage to look inward and acknowledge the parts of ourselves that we would rather keep hidden.

It is only through this self-reflection and self-acceptance that we can truly begin to heal. As we delve into the darkness of our past, we may find that there are areas of our lives that we have been avoiding or denying. We may have built up layers of defense mechanisms and coping strategies to protect ourselves from the pain, but these can ultimately prevent us from moving forward.

It is in these moments that we must be willing to let go of the attachments and beliefs that have been holding us back. We may need to challenge the negative self-talk and limiting beliefs that have been sabotaging our growth. We may need to confront the trauma or betrayal that has left us feeling broken and distrustful.

But as we do this work, we can also tap into the transformative power of the light of Jesus. Through prayer, meditation, and the guidance of the Holy Spirit, we can begin to see our lives and our experiences from a new perspective. Just as Joseph saw the greater good in his struggle during the famine. He comforted his brother by telling them that, yes, they meant it for evil but God meant it for good.

"As for you, you meant evil against me, but God meant it for good in order to bring about this present outcome, that many people would

> *be kept alive [as they are this day."*
> *(Genesis: 50:20)*

We can start to understand how our struggles have shaped us, and how they have ultimately brought us closer to God.

In the process of unraveling the threads of the past, we may also need to seek the support and guidance of others. This could come in the form of a trusted friend, a therapist, or a spiritual mentor. These individuals can provide us with the compassion, understanding, and accountability that we need to navigate the complexities of our past and move toward a brighter future.

As we engage in this process, it is important to remember that it is not a straight journey. There may be moments of progress and setbacks, of light and darkness. But with each step, we can grow in our understanding and our ability to navigate the challenges that arise.

Ultimately, the process of unraveling the threads of the past is not about dwelling in the darkness or wallowing in our failures. Rather, it is about embracing the light of Jesus and using it to transform our lives. It is about recognizing that our past experiences, no matter how painful, have the potential to be the very thing that propels us toward a deeper relationship with God and a more fulfilling life.

We can find wisdom and guidance in the words of the Apostle Paul, who wrote, *"Forgetting what is behind and straining toward what is ahead, I press on toward the goal to win the prize for which God has called me heavenward in Christ Jesus"* (Philippians 3:13-14). We need to realize the importance of leaving the past behind and focusing our energy on the future God has in store for us.

Our formative school years are like the foundational threads of our lives. The experiences we have during those years can leave permanent marks on our mentality, shaping our self-worth, self-esteem, and the beliefs we hold about ourselves.

One example is the impact of a classmate's cruel words. When someone calls you *"ugly,"* it can deeply affect your self-perception, leading to a lifetime of insecurity and self-doubt. Similarly, if someone comments on your appearance, telling you that you look obese or that you look like someone who has kwashiorkor. These words can have a profound impact on individuals struggling with weight-related issues. The sting of those words can linger, even into adulthood, and becomes triggers, driving us to engage in unhealthy behaviors, such as undereating, overeating, or even adding to our physical appearance, to *"prove"* our worth and silence the echoes of the past.

These limiting beliefs, forged in the early years of our childhood and adolescence, can continue to hold us back well into adulthood. They become the threads that bind us to the past, preventing us from fully embracing the present and reaching for the future. Moving forward and leaving behind the things that no longer serve us is a process with many painful yet liberating steps.

To move forward and leave behind the things that no longer serve us, we must first address the limiting beliefs cemented in our mentality in our formative years.

It's a process of unraveling the threads of the past, carefully examining the origins of our self-perceptions, and challenging the negative narratives we've internalized. The first step in unraveling the threads of the past is to develop self-awareness. This requires taking an honest, introspective look at our lives, and exploring the formative experiences, relationships, and beliefs that have molded us. It's about shedding light on the invisible scripts that have been running in the background, guiding our decisions, and shaping our sense of identity.

Activity: Reflect on your strongest convictions and write them in the table below as well as the event that left you with that conviction.

e.g.

Conviction: As a mother, I must always put my children's needs above mine.

Reasoning: I have always seen my mother put her need for food, clothing, and emotional support above our need for the same things.

CONVICTION	REASONING

Review the list above and identify the convictions that are limiting you or the ones that need to be addressed.

This journey of self-reflection and healing can be difficult, but it's a necessary step in the path to growth and self-actualization. By confronting the ghosts of your past, you can begin to rewrite the story, replacing the limiting beliefs with empowering ones. You can learn to see yourself not through the lens of others' perceptions, but through the lens of your worth and potential.

As you unravel the threads of the past, you open yourself up to the possibility of a brighter future. You can shed the shackles of self-doubt and embrace the person you were meant to become. It's a process of reclaiming your power, your voice, and your right to define yourself on your terms.

As you bring these unconscious patterns to the surface, you may be faced with difficult emotions, such as grief, shame, or regret. It's important to approach this process with compassion, remembering that the past has shaped you, but it does not define you. Through the lens of self-compassion, you can begin to untangle the threads, gently releasing the hold they have on your present and future.

The next step is to discern which threads are worth preserving and which ones need to go.

Some aspects of your past may still be serving you, providing a foundation of resilience, wisdom, or cherished memories. These are the threads you want to preserve, as they can be beneficial in our new life. However, some threads have become frayed, worn, or even toxic, keeping you fastened to outdated beliefs, unhealthy patterns, or limiting identities. These are the threads that need to be unraveled, creating space for the new to emerge.

This process of selective unraveling can be both liberating and overwhelming. It requires you to confront the parts of yourself that you may have been avoiding or denying, to face the fears and insecurities that have been holding you back.

But in doing so, you unlock the possibility of transformation, of weaving a new design that reflects your authentic self and the life we are called to live.

Throughout this journey, it's important to remember that unraveling the past is not about erasing or denying it. Rather, it's about acknowledging the role it has played in your life, honoring the lessons it has taught you, and then consciously choosing which threads to carry forward and which ones to let go of. The journey may not be easy, but the rewards are immeasurable.

As you courageously engage in this process, you may find yourself encountering the words of the prophet Isaiah, who declared, *"Forget the former things; do not dwell on the past. See, I am doing a new thing! Now it springs up; do you not perceive it?"* (Isaiah 43:18-19). This invitation to let go of the past and embrace the new work God is doing within you can provide a powerful source of hope and inspiration as you navigate the uncharted territory of your transformation.

What are the threads that need unraveling in your life?

Is it childhood trauma?

The wounds of childhood, whether they be emotional, physical, or sexual abuse, neglect, or other forms of trauma, can cast long shadows over an individual's life, shaping their beliefs, behaviors, and relationships well into adulthood. These deeply ingrained experiences of the past can become an invisible shackle, limiting one's ability to fully embrace the present and future.

To break free, individuals must embark on the difficult process of unpacking and unraveling the complex threads of their childhood trauma. This can involve intensive therapy, the cultivation of healthy coping mechanisms, and the gradual reclamation of their power. It requires a willingness to confront the painful memories and beliefs that have been shaped by the past and replace them with a newfound sense of self-worth, resilience, and compassion.

Is it an Addiction?

For those struggling with addiction, the past can be a minefield of triggers, trauma, and unhealthy coping mechanisms that perpetuate the cycle of abuse be it substance or otherwise. Whether it's the memory of traumatic events that led to the initial substance use, or the habits and social circles that have fueled the addiction, the past can be a challenging obstacle to achieving long-term recovery.

To break free, individuals in recovery must engage in the demanding process of unpacking and unraveling the complex web of experiences, beliefs, and behaviors that have kept them tethered to addiction. This can involve fasting and prayer, intensive therapy, support groups, and the cultivation of new, healthier habits and relationships that replace the old, destructive patterns.

It's a journey that requires immense courage, vulnerability, and a willingness to confront the painful truths of the past to forge a new, sober future. But for those who can successfully unravel the threads of their addiction-fueled past, the reward is the freedom to create a life of purpose, connection, and fulfillment.

Is it an abusive relationship?

For many people trapped in abusive relationships, the past can act as a powerful anchor, holding them in place even as the present becomes increasingly toxic and harmful. The emotional, psychological, and sometimes physical abuse they've endured over the years can create a deep sense of trauma, low self-worth, and an inability to envision a life beyond the confines of the relationship.

To break free, these individuals often need to engage in a painstaking process of unraveling the threads of the past - confronting the memories of abuse, challenging the internalized beliefs that have kept them feeling powerless, and rebuilding their sense of self-worth and autonomy. This can involve seeking therapy, surrounding themselves with a strong support system, and gradually reclaiming their independence and agency.

It's a difficult and courageous journey, but one that is essential for escaping the prison of an abusive relationship and creating a future free from the shadows of the past

Ultimately, unraveling the threads of the past is not a one-time event, but a lifelong journey of self-discovery and growth. It's a process of continually examining our beliefs, shedding outdated identities, and making space for the person we are becoming. By courageously engaging in this work, we unlock the possibility of living a more authentic life.

It is about embracing the light of Jesus and using it to transform our lives. It is about recognizing that our past experiences, no matter how painful, have the potential to be the very thing that propels us toward a deeper relationship with God and a more fulfilling life.

As we continue on this journey, we can take comfort in the knowledge that we are not alone. We are surrounded by a cloud of witnesses, both seen and unseen, who have walked this path before us. We can draw strength from the stories of those who have overcome their struggles and found the light of God's love shining through even the darkest of times.

In the end, the process of unraveling the threads of the past is not about perfection or achieving a state of flawlessness. It is about embracing our humanity, our imperfections, and our capacity for growth and transformation. It is about allowing the light of Jesus to illuminate our lives, not just in the moments of triumph, but amid our greatest challenges and difficulties.

So, let us continue to walk this path with courage, with vulnerability, and with the unwavering belief that the light of God's love will guide us through the shadows and into the fullness of life. Let us be willing to confront our skeletons, face the darkness, and allow the light of Jesus to illuminate our situation, knowing that it is in these moments of vulnerability and honesty that we can find the healing and wholeness we seek.

Chapter 5
Forgiveness
Unlocking New Beginnings

For a long time, I felt that the way my mother parented my siblings and I when we were younger was quite questionable. The things she would say to us still hurt me, even during my teenage and early adult years. This is a common experience that many of us go through with our parents.

I've come to realize that my parents were doing the best they could with the limited information and resources they had. My mother, for example, lost her mother at a very young age. When she was raising my three siblings and I, she was essentially a child raising children herself. She didn't have the benefit of modern-day support systems, like being able to call a friend and vent when she felt overwhelmed.

Instead, my mother had to rely on the little she knew about what it meant to be a mother and how to care for her children. And during her challenges and lack of support, she would often lash out at us when she felt overwhelmed. But through it all, she did her best to make sure we felt loved. She played and read to us, and ensured we had clean clothes and a clean home. She fed us and never once told us she didn't have something; she always made an effort.

Even in early adulthood, I often reflected on my younger years, and I disapproved of the way my mother did things. I did not understand why she acted the way she did. But then, one day, the Holy Spirit opened my eyes to the struggles my mother was facing as a person, not just as a mother. I realized that she had to put on her "superwoman cape" and do her best to serve us, despite the limited experience and examples she had. She had to deal with the immense childhood trauma she experienced, trying her best to not let us experience those traumas, especially in the magnitude she did. She had to pour into our jars of love from her jar that wasn't even a quarter full. Mommy, I salute you – you are truly a mother, and I now know that you did the best you could have done for us.

This realization led me to repent and start showing my mother more compassion. At that moment, I recognized that our leaders, including our parents, are not superheroes. They are not perfect, and they are also on their journey of growth and healing.

When we fail to acknowledge this, we can become quick to judge and criticize, rather than extend grace and forgiveness.

---

*Our leaders, **including our parents**, are not superheroes. They are not perfect; they are also on their journey of growth and healing.*

As I embraced this new perspective, I've learned the importance of having a forgiving spirit, especially towards those who have caused us pain or damage. It's easy to get stuck in the past and hold onto the scars and wounds that our parents' actions have left on us or those who were supposed to care for and nurture us. But when we peel away the bandages and look with eyes of compassion, we can begin to see the humanity in our parents and understand that they were doing the best they could with the little they had. This also extends far beyond our parents; it applies to that teacher who made you feel less than in grade school or that aunt or uncle who scarred you when you were younger. It extends to your first relationship and even to our church family and friends in our support system.

Forgiveness is not about excusing or condoning harmful behaviours. It's about releasing the resentment and bitterness that can weigh us down so that we can move forward and embrace the changes that come with this newfound understanding. By letting go of the past and embracing forgiveness, we open ourselves up to a future filled with healing, growth, and the possibility of reconciliation.

The Bible speaks to the power of forgiveness, reminding us to *"be kind and compassionate to one another, forgiving each other, just as in Christ God forgave you"* (Ephesians 4:32). When we extend the same grace and forgiveness that God has shown us to our parents and others who have hurt us, we can find freedom and a new perspective on the challenges of the past.

Embracing this change and letting go of the past is not always easy, but it is a necessary step in our journey of personal growth and wholeness. By doing so, we can release ourselves from the burden of resentment and open our hearts to the new opportunities that God has in store for us.

Forgiveness is a powerful tool that can help us navigate the changes and challenges life presents. Whether it's forgiving ourselves or others, the act of forgiveness can be transformative, allowing us to move forward and embrace the new opportunities that arise.

Often, the things and places that no longer serve us are a result of our past experiences, mistakes, and relationships. It's natural to feel a sense of attachment to or even resentment towards these aspects of our lives. However, it's important to remember that most people do the best they can with the information they have at the time.

Frequently, during our healing process, we are less hesitant to forgive those people who have hurt us but neglect to forgive ourselves. It is imperative in this journey of embracing change and leaving behind the things that no longer serve us that we forgive ourselves too. We have all sinned and have fallen short, and we have been redeemed through Jesus Christ, therefore, be quick not to condemn ourselves when it comes to our own mistakes and poor choices.

Many of us carry around the weight of our past, feeling depressed and guilty years later about things we've done. We replay those moments in our minds, wishing we could go back and change them. But just like Jesus said to the woman caught in adultery, "Where are your accusers?" The past is the past, and the only opinion that truly matters is God's.

And the good news is, that God is not condemning us. He looks at us with compassion and love, not judgment. He knows that we are all imperfect human beings, doing the best we can with the knowledge and resources we have. The mistakes we've made don't define us, and they don't have to hold us back from moving forward. Don't let your past mistakes absorb you to the point that you feel it define the rest of your life.

Don't get absorbed in your past mistakes, thinking it define the rest of your life.

It's time to release the guilt and shame we carry around. Failed relationships, the loss of a loved one - these things can weigh heavily on our hearts, but we must remember that they are not our fault and even if we think they were, what matters is the lesson we have learned that will help us to make better choices in the years to come. We can't control every outcome in life, and sometimes, things happen that are simply out of our hands.

Forgiving ourselves is the first step to true freedom. When we stop beating ourselves up over the past, we open ourselves up to the possibility of growth, healing, and new beginnings. We can learn from our mistakes, but we don't have to let them define us. God sees us as whole, worthy, and loved, and that's the only opinion that matters. So, let's extend the same grace to ourselves that we so freely give to others. Let's release the burden of the past and embrace the future, knowing that we are forgiven and loved, just as we are.

In the Bible, we find a powerful story of forgiveness that can inspire us to let go of the past and embrace the future. The story of the Prodigal Son, found in Luke 15:11-32, illustrates the power of forgiveness and acceptance.

The Prodigal Son, after squandering his inheritance, returns home, expecting to be rejected by his father. Instead, the father welcomes him with open arms, celebrating his return and forgiving him for his past mistakes. This story reminds us that no matter how far we may have strayed, there is always the possibility of forgiveness and a fresh start.

As we reflect on this biblical story, let us consider three key verses that can guide us on our journey of forgiveness and change:

1. "Be kind and compassionate to one another, forgiving each other, just as in Christ God forgave you." (Ephesians 4:32)
2. "If we confess our sins, he is faithful and just and will forgive us our sins and purify us from all unrighteousness." (1 John 1:9)
3. "Forget the former things; do not dwell on the past. See, I am doing a new thing! Now it springs up; do you not perceive it?" (Isaiah 43:18-19)

Remember, God's grace and forgiveness are always available to us. When we confess our sins and ask for forgiveness, He is faithful to forgive us and cleanse us from all unrighteousness (1 John 1:9). This knowledge can give us the courage to forgive ourselves, knowing that we are loved and accepted by God, despite our imperfections.

Forgiving others can be one of the most challenging aspects of the forgiveness process. When someone has hurt us, it's natural to feel anger, resentment, and a desire for vengeance. However, holding onto these negative emotions can be detrimental to our own well-being and personal growth.

The Bible reminds us to "be kind and compassionate to one another, forgiving each other, just as in Christ God forgave you" (Ephesians 4:32). This verse encourages us to extend the same grace and forgiveness that we have received from God to those who have wronged us. Even when someone's actions have caused us pain, they may have been acting out of their hurt, fear, or lack of understanding. By recognizing their humanity and extending compassion, we can begin the process of forgiveness and release ourselves from the burden of resentment.

When we forgive ourselves and others, we create space for growth and transformation.

As we navigate the process of forgiveness, we must also be willing to embrace the changes that come with it. The things and places that no longer serve us may be remnants of our past, holding us back from fully living in the present and embracing the future.

The prophet Isaiah reminds us, *"Forget the former things; do not dwell on the past. See, I am doing a new thing! Now it springs up; do you not perceive it?"* (Isaiah 43:18-19). This verse encourages us to let go of the past and be open to the new things God is doing in our lives.

When we forgive ourselves and others, we create space for growth and transformation. We can let go of the things and places that no longer serve us and embrace the new opportunities that arise. This can be a challenging process, but it is also a liberating one, as we free ourselves from the weight of the past and open ourselves to the possibilities of the future.

As we move forward, let us embrace change with courage and an open heart. Let us forgive ourselves for our past mistakes and extend the same grace to those who have hurt us. In doing so, we can find freedom, healing, and the chance to create a better future, one filled with the blessings and possibilities that God has in store for us

Chapter 6
Let it Go
Forgetting the Injustices

"I forgive, but I won't forget" is a common attitude that reflects a desire to hold onto the hurt and pain of the past. While forgiveness is a crucial step in the healing process, it is not enough on its own. True freedom comes when we can let go of the negative experiences that we had, allowing ourselves to move forward without the weight of the past holding us back. The process of letting go is essential for personal growth, healing, and the ability to move forward in a meaningful way.

We convince ourselves that by holding onto the memory of the injustice committed against us, we are somehow protecting ourselves from being hurt again. We think that by never letting go of what was done to us, we are maintaining control and ensuring it never happens again. But the reality is that this mindset is incredibly damaging - both to ourselves and our relationships with others.

True forgiveness requires letting go, not just of the wrongdoing, but of the need to hold onto the memory of it forever. It means wiping the slate clean, releasing the anger and hurt, and choosing to move forward without the baggage of the past. God Himself promises to cast our sins into the sea of forgetfulness - to completely erase them and give us a fresh start. Is the servant greater than its master?

Yet so often, we struggle to extend that same grace to those who have wronged us. We say the words "I forgive you," but we hold tight to the memory of the offence, unwilling to truly let it go. We tell ourselves that by never forgetting, we are protecting ourselves - but in reality, we are only trapping ourselves in the past, unable to move forward.

Imagine you are walking down the street, texting on your phone, and suddenly you trip over a broken tree limb on the sidewalk. You fall hard, scraping your knee and elbow. It hurts, and you're understandably angry at whoever is responsible for the limb being there. But rather than simply getting back up, dusting yourself off, and continuing your way, you decide to stand there, kicking and cursing the limb on the sidewalk. "I'll never forget how you made me fall and messed up my clothes!" "I'm going to remember this moment forever, and every time I walk by here, I'll be reminded of the pain you caused me.

Ridiculous, right? Yet that's often exactly how we handle the hurts and injustices we face in our lives. We refuse to let go, stubbornly clinging to the memory of the wrong that was done to us. We replay the hurtful event over and over in our minds, unable to move past it. And in doing so, we end up punishing ourselves far more than we punish the one who wronged us.

When we hold onto past hurts, we give those hurts power over us. We allow them to shape our present and future, tainting our relationships and decision-making. The person who hurt us may have long since moved on, yet we remain anchored in the past, our lives and emotions still controlled by their actions. It's as if we're constantly re-injuring ourselves, picking at a scab that should have healed long ago.

Psychologists have a term for this phenomenon: **rumination.** *Rumination is the tendency to repetitively think about the causes, situational factors, and consequences of one's negative emotional experience.* In other words, it's the act of obsessively dwelling on past hurts and injustices. Studies have shown that rumination is closely linked to increased feelings of depression, anxiety, and even physical health problems. The more we dwell on our past wounds, the deeper they seem to cut.

Letting go of those wounds, on the other hand, can have a profound and transformative effect. When we truly forgive and release the hurt someone has caused us, we free ourselves from the emotional baggage of the past. We stop giving that person and that event power over our lives. We can move forward with joy, positivity, and a sense of inner peace.

It's not easy, of course. Forgiveness is one of the hardest things we are called to do as human beings. When we've been deeply wounded, whether emotionally, physically, or spiritually, the natural instinct is to protect ourselves by holding onto that pain.

Imagine a different scenario. You're walking down the street, and you trip over that same broken tree limb on the sidewalk. This time, however, instead of glaring at it and vowing to never forget, you simply get back up, brush yourself off, and continue your way. The limb is still there and the fact that you messed up your clothes as a result of it remains, but you've chosen not to let it ruin your day or define your future interactions with that stretch of pavement. You recognized it as a one-time event, an unfortunate accident, and you didn't allow it to consume you or dictate your actions going forward.

That's the power of true forgiveness. When we let go of the need to hold onto past wrongs, we free ourselves to live in the present moment. We stop giving our energy and attention to something that has already happened and can't be changed. Instead, we focus on the here and now, on how we can move forward in a positive, productive way.

Of course, that's easier said than done. Forgiveness doesn't happen overnight, and it's not a one-and-done event. It's an ongoing process, a daily choice to release the hurt and pain, even when it feels impossible. But the rewards of that choice are immense.

When we forgive, we not only free ourselves from the weight of the past, but we open the door to deeper, more meaningful relationships in the present. Holding onto resentment and bitterness erects barriers between us and others, making it difficult to truly connect. But when we let go and choose forgiveness, we create space for empathy, understanding, and reconciliation.

Think about a time when you've been deeply hurt by someone close to you - a friend, family member, or romantic partner. The natural response is to pull away, to shut them out, and to protect ourselves from further pain. But what happens when we take that approach? The relationship becomes strained, the trust is broken, and the bond between us and the other person weakens. We might think we're keeping ourselves safe, but in reality, we're just cutting ourselves off from the very thing that could help us heal which is a genuine connection.

On the other hand, when we choose forgiveness - even when it's incredibly difficult - we open the door to restoration and healing. We recognize that the other person is human, that they too are flawed and imperfect. We extend grace, allowing them the opportunity to make amends and rebuild trust. And in doing so, we not only strengthen our relationship with them, but we also experience a profound sense of inner peace and freedom.

Forgiveness is a powerful antidote to the poisons of resentment, anger, and bitterness. When we let go of the need to hold onto past wrongs, we free ourselves to move forward with hope, joy, and a renewed sense of purpose. We stop allowing our lives to be defined by the hurt we've experienced and instead focus on the beauty, the goodness, and the possibilities that lie ahead.

This doesn't mean that the pain of the past simply disappears or that we never think about it again. Trauma and injustice leave scars, and those scars can take time to heal. But when we choose forgiveness, we stop picking at those scars, allowing them to mend properly. We acknowledge the hurt, we mourn the loss, and then we make the conscious choice to move on.

I once saw a reel on Instagram, that told the story of the two wolves. An old Cherokee is teaching his grandson about life, and he says, "A fight is going on inside me. It is a terrible fight, and it is between two wolves. One wolf is evil - he is anger, envy, sorrow, regret, greed, arrogance, self-pity, guilt, resentment, inferiority, lies, false pride, superiority, and ego." He continued, "The other is good - he is joy, peace, love, hope, serenity, humility, kindness, benevolence, empathy, generosity, truth, compassion, and faith. The same fight is going on inside you - and inside every other person, too."

The grandson thought about it for a minute and then asked, "Grandfather, which wolf will win?"

The old Cherokee simply replied, "The one you feed."

That's the power of forgiveness. When we choose to let go of the past and focus on feeding the good wolf within us - the one of love, peace, and compassion - we starve the evil wolf of resentment, bitterness, and unforgiveness. We shift our energy away from dwelling on past hurts and toward creating a brighter, more fulfilling future.

It's not always easy, of course. Forgetting past hurts requires a willingness to be vulnerable. It means acknowledging our imperfections and shortcomings and extending the same grace to others that we hope to receive. But the rewards are immense.

When we choose to forget, we free ourselves from the emotional and spiritual bondage of the past. We stop allowing our lives to be dictated by the whims and actions of others, and instead take control of our destiny. We become more resilient, more adaptable, and more capable of weathering the storms of life.

And perhaps most importantly, we open ourselves up to deeper, more meaningful relationships. When we let go of the need to hold onto past hurts, we stop using our wounds as a shield to keep others at a distance and instead allow ourselves to be vulnerable and fully present in our interactions.

Imagine a scenario where you've been deeply hurt by someone you care about. Instead of immediately shutting them out and vowing never to forgive them, take a step back and try to see the situation from their perspective. What might have been going on in their life that led them to act in that way? Is it possible that they themselves were struggling with their pain or trauma? Can you find it in your heart to extend them the same grace and compassion that you hope to receive?

It's not always easy, but when we make that conscious choice to forgive, the benefits are amazing. We free ourselves from the shackles of the past and open ourselves up to a brighter, future. We stop allowing our lives to be defined by the hurt we've experienced and instead focus on the beauty, the joy, and the potential that lies ahead.

So let go of the need to hold onto past wrongs. Forgive those who have hurt you, not for their sake, but for your own. Allow yourself to let go of the anger, the resentment, and the bitterness, and instead choose love, empathy, and understanding. It's a journey, to be sure, but one that is well worth the effort.

After all, as the Bible says in Micah 7:19, *"[God] will again have compassion on us; he will tread our iniquities underfoot. You will cast all our sins into the depths of the sea."* If God Himself is willing to forgive us and cast our sins into the sea of forgetfulness, surely, we can do the same for those who have wronged us. Let go of the past and embrace the freedom and healing that true forgiveness brings.

Chapter 7
Breaking out of limiting Beliefs

One of the most crucial steps in moving on from the past and embracing a new future is the process of breaking free from our limiting beliefs. These deeply ingrained thought patterns and self-perceptions often serve as the invisible shackles that keep us fastened to the familiar, even when it no longer serves our highest good.

Throughout our lives, we accumulate a lifetime's worth of experiences, influences, and societal conditioning that shape the way we view ourselves and the world around us. All too often, these belief systems become a prison of our own making, confining us to a narrow, self-limiting existence that falls far short of our true potential.

Perhaps you grew up with the belief that you weren't *"smart enough"* to pursue higher education, or that your economic background meant you were destined for a life of struggle.

Maybe you've held onto the notion that you're *"not the type of person"* who takes risks or chases big dreams. These limiting beliefs can manifest in countless ways, subtly sabotaging our efforts at every turn.

Limiting beliefs can be a significant obstacle to our personal and professional growth. One prime example of a limiting belief that many people struggle with is the *"that's just how it is"* mentality. This mindset often stems from observing the patterns and behaviours of our immediate social circles, such as our family members or community.

Imagine a young person growing up in a family where the traditional career path has always been to pursue a stable, government job. Their parents and grandparents have all followed this route, and the idea of exploring alternative career options has never been entertained. This individual might find themselves thinking, "This is how I saw my grandmother, mother, and everyone before did it, so that's how I did it".

This mindset can be incredibly limiting, as it prevents the individual from considering the vast array of possibilities that may be available to them. They may feel trapped in a predetermined path, unable to envision a future that deviates from the well-worn patterns of their past.

The "this is how I am; I don't have any change to change " mentality is another example of a limiting belief that can hinder personal growth. They overemphasize the fact that they have always been the way they are, they have always done things the way they are doing them, and they will not do things differently. If something works why fix it, right?

Their situation shows that their method is not working for them. Consider a hot-tempered individual who had to change jobs every three to six months because they kept getting into altercations with other employees. This person may feel like, that's just how I am, and I will not tolerate anyone speaking to me a certain type of way, and anyone that says something that I don't like I'm most definitely giving him or her a piece of my mind. Even though that mindset is not working in their favor they keep doing the same thing over and over. They have been doing the same thing expecting a different result. The truth is not everyone will say the right words in the right tone at all times but sometimes we have to be the bigger person, exercise grace, and look beyond the faults of others. We can tactfully express our dissatisfaction regarding the matter. Let us not use the "that's how I am" mentality as a crutch and remain stuck when we can embrace the new and live a liberated life.

This mindset reflects a sense of acceptance, where the individual feels that they are powerless to change their circumstances or break out of the mold that has been set for them.

This type of limiting belief can have far-reaching consequences, as it can lead to a lack of motivation, reduced self-confidence, and a reluctance to take risks or try new things. It can also perpetuate a cycle of stagnation, where the individual remains stuck in a state of complacency, unable to explore their full potential

Another crippling belief is that "when God is ready, He will heal me." This perspective places the responsibility outside of our own hands, disempowering us from taking the necessary steps of faith to walk in wholeness.

In the book of Mark, we read the powerful account of the woman with the issue of blood who reached out and touched Jesus. The Scripture states that *"as *many as touched Him were made whole"* (Mark 6:56). The emphasis here is not on how many He touched, but on how many reached out to touch Him. The woman took an active role in her healing, rather than passively waiting for Jesus to heal her.

Instead of placing the responsibility on God, the woman reached out in faith, taking hold of the healing that was rightfully hers.

Some time ago, I made a tumbler for my friend, to celebrate her last chemo dose. I called her and told her I made the tumbler and showed her a picture as well. Her name was printed on it along with a victory message. She told me she was coming for it, and she liked it a lot. Days turned into weeks and weeks turned into a month before she came to collect it. That tumbler was hers, and all she had to do was to reach out and collect what was rightfully hers.

It is the same where our healing is concerned. All we must do is reach out in faith and grab what is rightfully ours. The Bible declares that "by His stripes, we are healed" (Isaiah 53:5). Healing is part of the finished work of Christ on the cross - it is our inheritance as children of God. As the Scripture says, healing is the "children's bread" (Matthew 15:26) - it is God's will and desire for His children to walk in divine health and wholeness.

By His stripes we are healed"

Isaiah 53:5

To break free from the limiting belief of being anchored to past beliefs, we must make a conscious choice to let go and move forward. This requires us to repent of any self-pity, unforgiveness, or negative mindsets that have kept us chained to the past. We must renew our minds with the truth of God's Word, which declares that we are new creations in Christ and that the old has passed away (2 Corinthians 5:17).

As we do this, we will be empowered to reach out in faith, like the woman with the issue of blood, and take hold of the healing that has already been provided. We must stop waiting for God to do something and start believing, receiving, and actively participating in our restoration.

Healing is not something we have to convince God to do - it is something we must believe, receive, and walk in by faith. When we let go of the past and step out in bold, expectant faith, we will experience the fullness of God's restorative power in our lives. The past no longer has to define us; we can step into the abundant life that Christ has made available to us.

The process of breaking free from these mental shackles can be overwhelming. It requires a willingness to step out of our comfort zones, to question the narratives we've clung to for so long, and to courageously confront the fears that have held us back. But make no mistake - it is an essential step in the journey of personal growth and transformation.

To break free from these limiting beliefs, it's essential to challenge the underlying assumptions and narratives that have shaped our perspectives. This may involve seeking out new experiences, surrounding ourselves with people who have achieved success in unconventional ways, and actively questioning the validity of the beliefs that have been ingrained in us.

It's also important to recognize that just because something has been done a certain way in the past doesn't mean it's the only way or the best way. The world is constantly evolving, and what may have worked for our grandparents or parents may not necessarily be the right path for us.

One of the keyways to begin this process is through the practice of self-awareness. By taking the time to deeply examine our thoughts, emotions, and behaviors, we can start to uncover the root causes of our limiting beliefs. Perhaps you'll discover that the fear of failure stems from a childhood experience of being criticized, or that your belief in your unworthiness originated from the limiting messages you received from well-meaning but misguided loved ones.

Once we've shone a light on these deeply held beliefs, the real work begins. It's time to challenge those narratives, to actively replace them with new, empowering perspectives. This might involve affirmations, visualization exercises, or simply surrounding ourselves with people and environments that reinforce our sense of possibility.

It's important to remember that this is not a one-time event, but rather an ongoing process of self-discovery and personal evolution. Our limiting beliefs can be deeply entrenched, and it may take time and consistent effort to truly uproot them. But with each step forward, we'll find ourselves standing a little taller, our vision a little clearer, and our sense of what's possible expanding exponentially.

And as we break free from the mental and emotional constraints that have been holding us back, we open the door to a world of new opportunities. We can finally step out of the gilded cage of the past and into the boundless potential of the future, unencumbered by the weight of our self-imposed limitations.

It's a journey that requires courage, vulnerability, and a deep commitment to our own growth. But the rewards are truly transformative. By shedding the layers of limiting beliefs, we reclaim our power, our purpose, and our ability to create the life we've always dreamed of. And in doing so, we unlock the door to a future that is truly our own.

Chapter 8
Stay Teachable

In a world that is always changing, it can be tempting to hold onto the familiar and avoid growth. Many people find comfort in the traditions and beliefs they were raised with, and the idea of letting go of those things can be scary. However, the ability to stay teachable - to remain open-minded, humble, and willing to learn - is essential for personal and spiritual growth.

When we anchor ourselves in the past and refuse to embrace change, we risk becoming stuck and irrelevant. The Bible reminds us that *"the one who is unwilling to change is unwilling to grow"* (2 Corinthians 3:18). To truly prosper, we must be willing to let go of the things that no longer help us and open ourselves up to new perspectives, ideas, and ways of being.

The book of Proverbs tells us that *"Whoever loves discipline loves knowledge, but whoever hates correction is stupid"* (Proverbs 12:1). This shows us the importance of staying teachable - of being willing to receive instruction, feedback, and guidance, even when it is uncomfortable or challenges our existing beliefs. It is only through this willingness to learn that we can grow and evolve.

"Whoever loves discipline loves knowledge, but whoever hates correction is stupid" (Proverbs 12:1).

One key part of staying teachable is maintaining a humble spirit. The Bible warns against the dangers of pride, which can blind us to our need for growth and learning. Proverbs 16:18 reminds us that "Pride goes before destruction, a haughty spirit before a fall." When we are full of pride and arrogance, we become resistant to change and closed off to the insights and wisdom of others.

The Bible praises the virtues of humility. Proverbs 11:2 states that, *"when pride comes, then comes disgrace, but with humility comes wisdom."* When we approach life with a humble, open-minded spirit, we create space for learning and growth. We become more willing to accept feedback, admit our mistakes, and explore new ideas and perspectives.

This is not to say that staying teachable means giving up all of our core beliefs and values. It is important to have a strong foundation of principles, and moral standards that guide us. However, it is also vital that we remain open to new ways of understanding and applying those beliefs.

The Bible encourages us to *"test everything; hold fast to what is good"* (1 Thessalonians 5:21). This suggests that we should not just blindly accept everything we are taught, but rather, we should think critically and discern what resonates with us.

One of the challenges of staying teachable is that it can be uncomfortable and painful at times. When we are confronted with new information or perspectives that challenge our existing beliefs, it can be tempting to become defensive or resistant. However, the Bible reminds us that "the wise are open to correction" (Proverbs 12:15) and that "the one who listens to a life-giving rebuke will be at home among the wise" (Proverbs 15:31).

"The wise are open to correction"

(Proverbs 12:15)

This means we must be willing to humble ourselves, admit our mistakes, and embrace the discomfort of growth and change. It is only through this willingness to be vulnerable and open to correction that we can truly deepen our understanding and move forward in a meaningful way.

Another key part of staying teachable is the ability to let go of the things that no longer serve us. In the book of Ecclesiastes, we are reminded that "there is a time for everything, and a season for every activity under the heavens" (Ecclesiastes 3:1). This suggests that the things that may have been important or meaningful to us in the past may no longer be relevant or helpful in the present.

When we cling to the past and refuse to let go of the things that no longer serve us, we can become weighed down and held back from growth and progress. The Bible warns against the dangers of holding onto the past, reminding us that *"the former things will not be remembered, nor will they come to mind"* (Isaiah 65:17).

Instead, we are encouraged to embrace change and be willing to let go of the things that no longer serve us. In the book of Philippians, Paul writes: *"But one thing I do: Forgetting what is behind and straining toward what is ahead, I press on toward the goal to win the prize for which God has called me heavenward in Christ Jesus"* (Philippians 3:13-14).

This speaks to the importance of staying focused on the present and the future, rather than dwelling on the past. When we can let go of the things that no longer serve us, we create space for new and exciting possibilities to emerge.

One of the key benefits of staying teachable is that it allows us to adapt and thrive in a rapidly changing world. The Bible reminds us that "the wise store up knowledge, but the mouth of a fool invites ruin" (Proverbs 10:14). When we can stay open-minded and learn from our experiences, we become better equipped to handle the challenges and opportunities that come our way. When we are unwilling to learn and grow, we risk making poor decisions and missing out on important insights and opportunities.

Staying teachable also allows us to deepen our faith and our connection with God. The Bible tells us that "whoever does not receive the kingdom of God like a child shall not enter it" (Mark 10:15). This suggests that the ability to approach life with a childlike sense of wonder and openness is essential for growth and transformation. When we are willing to learn and grow, we create space for God to work in our lives in new and profound ways. We become more receptive to the guidance and wisdom of the Holy Spirit, and we are better able to discern God's will for our lives.

In the book of James, we are reminded that *"if any of you lacks wisdom, you should ask God, who gives generously to all without finding fault, and it will be given to you"* (James 1:5). This speaks to the importance of being willing to seek out and receive the wisdom and guidance of God, even when it challenges our existing beliefs.

Ultimately, the ability to stay teachable is a powerful and essential tool for personal and spiritual growth. When we are willing to let go of the things that no longer serve us, choose to embrace change and new perspectives, and remain humble and open-minded, we create space for transformation and fulfillment.

The Bible offers us many examples of individuals who embodied this spirit of teachability, and who were able to grow and thrive as a result. One such example is the apostle Paul, who, before his conversion, was a zealous persecutor of the early Christian church. However, after encountering the risen Christ on the road to Damascus, Paul underwent a profound transformation, becoming one of the most influential advocates for the Christian faith. Paul's story can be found in Acts 9:1-19. Despite his deep-seated beliefs and convictions, Paul was willing to let go of his past and embrace a new way of thinking and being. He was open to the guidance and wisdom of the Holy Spirit, and he was not afraid to challenge his assumptions and preconceptions.

In his letter to the Philippians, Paul writes about the importance of forgetting "what is behind" and "straining toward what is ahead" (Philippians 3:13-14). This speaks to his willingness to let go of the past and embrace the opportunities for growth and transformation that lay before him.

Ultimately, the call to stay teachable is a call to embrace the fullness of our humanity and to recognize our need for growth and change. It is a call to let go of the things that no longer serve us, to be willing to admit our mistakes and shortcomings, and to approach life with a spirit of humility and openness.

As we traverse the complexities of the modern world, it is more important than ever to stay grounded in the wisdom and guidance of the past, while also remaining open to the new perspectives and insights that can help us to grow and evolve. By staying teachable, we can find the courage and resilience to embrace change, to let go of the things that no longer serve us, and to move forward with a renewed sense of purpose and direction.

Chapter 9
Take Responsibility
Embrace the power of choice

It's all too easy to look at our current circumstances and point fingers, blaming others for the challenges we face. We like to see ourselves as the heroes in our own stories, forgetting that every hero is a villain in someone else's narrative. Instead of taking responsibility for the choices we've made, we often choose to play the role of the victim, comforting ourselves with excuses and waiting for someone else to swoop in and save the day.

But the harsh reality is that we are where we are today because of the decisions we've made, both good and bad. The person we have become is a direct result of the steps we've taken, and the paths we've chosen to walk down. While it's understandable to feel frustrated when we feel like we haven't received the help or support we need from those around us, the truth is that we can't control the actions of others. The only thing we can control is our response to the circumstances we find ourselves in.

Think of it like this: imagine a young person who dreams of becoming a successful entrepreneur. They might look at their peers who come from wealthy families, who have the financial resources and connections to help them get their business off the ground and feel resentful. "If only my parents had been more supportive, or had the means to help me out," they might think to themselves. "Then I'd be where they are now."

I could have chosen to play the blame game, putting the responsibility for my attaining success according to societal standards on someone else. I could have chosen to blame my parents for not planning financially for my journey after high school. I saw the students I graduated from high school with obtaining their first degrees and doing things I had hoped to achieve at their age, but I took responsibility and planned accordingly to reach my goals. In the same breath, let me just say; that life is a race, but you are only in competition with the you of yesterday. You are not in competition with anyone else but you. Free yourself from the time stamps that society has imposed upon you, brainwashing you into believing if you don't achieve certain things by a certain age, you miss the mark. Progress is progress no matter how small, the only thing that matters is that you keep growing and never lose sight of where you are going.

The reality is that the path to success is rarely a straight line. Those who have achieved greatness have often had to overcome significant obstacles and challenges along the way. The ones who ultimately succeed are the ones who take responsibility for their actions, who refuse to be defined by their circumstances, and who are willing to put in the hard work and make the difficult choices necessary to reach their goals.

In the Bible, we see a powerful example of this in the story of Joseph. Sold into slavery by his brothers, Joseph could have easily become a bitter, resentful individual, blaming his family for the hardships he faced. But instead, he chose to take responsibility for his own life and trust in God's plan for him. Through his unwavering faith and resilience, Joseph rose to a position of power in Egypt and was ultimately able to save his family from famine.

"You intended to harm me, but God intended it for good to accomplish what is now being done, the saving of many lives."
(Genesis 50:20)

This verse from the book of Genesis serves as a powerful reminder that even during our darkest moments, when it feels like the world is against us, we have the power to choose how we respond. Joseph could have remained stuck in the past, dwelling on the betrayal of his brothers and the unfairness of his circumstances. Instead, he chose to see the bigger picture, to trust in God's plan, and to use his experiences to bring about something good.

Similarly, when we take responsibility for our own lives, when we stop making excuses and start to act, we open ourselves up to the possibility of transformation and growth. It's easy to sit back and complain about the hand we've been dealt, to point fingers at those who haven't helped us as much as we would have liked. But the truth is, no one is going to swoop in and save us – the only person who can truly change the trajectory of our lives is ourselves.

Think about the able-bodied individuals who complain that their families aren't making them a priority or aren't providing enough assistance. While it's understandable to feel frustrated, the reality is that most family members are struggling themselves, particularly if they have children of their own to care for. They're trying to put the pieces in place to create a better future for their own kids, and it's not their responsibility to shoulder the entire burden of supporting their adult family members.

Instead of waiting for someone else to step in and solve our problems, we need to take ownership of our own lives and start taking concrete steps towards the future we want to create. This might mean going back to school, even if it's difficult and uncomfortable. It might mean starting a side hustle or freelance business to supplement our income. It might mean making tough choices and sacrifices to pursue our dreams.

The bottom line is that at the end of the day, we won't be judged by who didn't help us, but by what we did to help ourselves. And when we take responsibility for our own lives, when we stop making excuses and start taking action, we open ourselves up to a world of possibilities.

The choice is ours to make. And it's a choice we have to make every single day, in the big decisions and the small ones. But when we embrace the power of choice, when we take responsibility for our lives, we unlock the door to a future that is brighter, more fulfilling, and more in line with the person we were created to be.

God will help us to fulfill our destiny but even with God's help, the responsibility ultimately rests on our shoulders. We must be willing to take the first step, to make the difficult choices, to put in the hard work required to see the change we want to see in our lives. And when we do, we'll find that the path forward becomes clearer, the obstacles start to shrink, and the future starts to look brighter and more promising.

So, let's stop making excuses, let's stop playing the victim, and let's start taking responsibility for our own lives. Let's embrace the power of choice, the power to shape our destiny, and let's start walking the path that leads to the future we were created to live.

Chapter 10
Embracing the Growth Mindset

A very good friend of mine, a former practising pharmacist turned elite financial advisor, serves as a shining example of the power of the growth mindset. Her journey is a testament to the transformative power of embracing the belief that our abilities and talents are not fixed, but can be cultivated and expanded through dedication, effort, and a willingness to take on new challenges.

For years, she had been content, or so it seemed, working as a pharmacist. She had a stable job, a respectable salary, and the respect of her colleagues. But deep down, she felt an overwhelming sense of dissatisfaction. The monotony of her daily routine, the confinement of being behind a desk, and the lack of fulfillment in her work had left her feeling unfulfilled and yearning for something more.

Initially, she resisted the idea of making a change. The thought of starting over in a new field filled her with anxiety and self-doubt. "I've already invested so much time and effort into this career path," she would tell herself. "It would be a waste to just throw it all away."

However, as She observed her colleagues who had embraced a growth mindset, the tide began to shift. She noticed that these individuals were the ones who seemed the most content and successful. They were the ones who weren't afraid to take risks, to learn new skills, and to push the boundaries of what was possible.

Inspired by their example, she decided to take a hard look at her own beliefs and assumptions. She realized that her fear of change was holding her back, that she had been limiting herself to a narrow set of options. With a newfound determination, she began to explore the idea of turning her side hustle into her full-time job, she took the leap and started focusing on the financial services industry.

The transition was not an easy one. I'm sure there were moments when she had to confront her doubts and insecurities, questioning whether she had what it took to make a successful transition. But with each step she took, her confidence grew. She enrolled in *'The Holy Ghost University'*, attended industry events, and reached out to professionals in the field for advice and mentorship.

Something remarkable happened as She immersed herself in this process of growth and self-discovery. She began to see the world in a new light, recognizing opportunities where she had once only seen obstacles. Her mind expanded, and she found herself embracing new ways of thinking and problem-solving.

Ultimately, J's journey led her to a fulfilling career as a financial advisor. She found that her pharmacist training and experience were not liabilities, but rather assets that she could leverage in new and exciting ways. Her deep understanding of the healthcare industry, her attention to detail, and her unwavering commitment to helping others made her a natural fit for the financial services sector.

Today, she is thriving in her new role as a financial advisor. She is no longer confined to the four walls of a pharmacy, but rather, she is traveling the world, meeting with clients, and helping them achieve their financial goals. Her passion for her work is profound, and her success is a testament to the power of the growth mindset.

J's story powerfully reminds us that the only way to truly leave behind what no longer serves us is to embrace the possibility of growth. By letting go of the limiting beliefs and fixed mindsets that hold us back, we open ourselves up to a world of new opportunities, fresh perspectives, and personal fulfillment.

The lesson of J's journey is that the growth mindset is not just a theoretical concept, but a practical tool for transformation. It is a mindset that empowers us to take on challenges, to learn from our mistakes, and to continuously evolve and improve. It is a mindset that allows us to break free from the constraints of the past and create a future that is aligned with our deepest values and aspirations. As we reflect on her story, let us be inspired to adopt the growth mindset in our own lives. Let us embrace the courage to step outside our comfort zones, take risks, and continuously expand the boundaries of our potential. It is only through this process of growth and self-discovery that we can truly leave behind what no longer serves us and create the life we've always dreamed of.

Embracing a Growth Mindset: A Self-Reflection

Take a few moments to reflect on your current mindset and how it affects your approach to challenges, learning, and personal growth. Answer the following questions honestly and thoughtfully:

1. When faced with a new challenge or task, what is your initial reaction? Do you feel excited to take it on and learn something new, or do you feel inclined to avoid it or give up easily?

----

2. How do you typically respond to setbacks or failures? Do you view them as opportunities to improve and try new strategies, or do you get discouraged and give up?

----

3. When you receive feedback or constructive criticism, how do you respond? Do you see it as a chance to identify areas for growth, or do you become defensive and dismiss it?

4. Do you believe that your abilities, skills, and intelligence are fixed, or do you see them as flexible and capable of development through effort and persistence?

---

5. When you encounter a challenge that seems beyond your current abilities, how do you

react? Do you shy away from it, or do you embrace the opportunity to stretch and grow?

If your responses indicate that you tend to have a more fixed mindset, don't worry. The good news is that a growth mindset can be cultivated and developed over time. Here are some steps you can take to start embracing a growth mindset:

1. Reframe your perspective on challenges and setbacks. Instead of seeing them as threats, view them as opportunities to learn and improve.

2. Seek out feedback and constructive criticism and use it as a tool for personal development.
3. Believe in your ability to grow and develop your skills through hard work and persistence.
4. Celebrate your progress and focus on the process rather than the result.
5. Surround yourself with people who have a growth mindset and can support and encourage you in your journey.

Remember, a growth mindset is not something you're born with; it's a mindset that can be learned and practiced. By embracing this perspective, you'll be better equipped to tackle challenges, learn and grow, and achieve your full potential.

Rebuilding the Foundation

Imagine building a house with all the necessary materials – the lumber, the bricks, the roofing tiles – but never actually putting them together. The materials may be there, but without taking the active steps to construct the foundation, frame the walls, and complete the structure, the house will never become a reality. It remains a mere idea, a potential that never reaches its full expression.

Similarly, the process of personal growth and transformation is like building a house. We may have the desire to change, the vision of the person we want to become, and even the resources and knowledge to get there. But unless we take the active steps to put that vision into practice, we'll remain stuck in the same patterns, unable to move forward. It is not enough to fall in love with the idea of growth, you have to be an active participant.

When God called Noah to build an ark in preparation for a great flood, Noah could have easily dismissed the idea, he could have said it was too difficult a task. But instead, he rolled up his sleeves and got to work, trusting in God's plan and taking the necessary steps to bring it to fruition.

> *"Noah did everything just as God commanded him." (Genesis 6:22)*

This simple yet profound verse highlights the importance of taking action, even when the task ahead seems challenging. Noah didn't just think about building the ark; he did it, one plank at a time, until the entire structure was complete.

In the same way, if we want to leave the past behind and embrace a new chapter in our lives, we can't afford to be spectators, just watching the story of our lives unfold left totally up to chance. We must be willing to take the first step, to stretch ourselves beyond our comfort zones, and to actively work towards the transformation we desire.

Consider the process of a seed becoming a tree. When a seed is planted in the ground, it doesn't simply sit there and wait for a tree to magically appear. Instead, it undergoes a remarkable transformation, sending down roots and pushing up through the soil to reach towards the sun.

This process requires the seed to take action – to break open, to grow, to stretch, and to adapt to its new environment. If the seed remains passive, it will never fulfill its potential and become the majestic tree it was meant to be.

In the same way, if we want to leave the past behind and embrace a new future, we must be willing to take action, break out of our old patterns, and stretch ourselves in new and unfamiliar ways. It's not enough to simply think about change; we must be willing to do the hard work of making it happen.

This may involve setting clear goals and taking concrete steps towards achieving them, whether that means going back to school, starting a new career, or addressing unresolved emotional issues. It may mean seeking out the support of a counselor, a mentor, or a community of like-minded individuals who can help us stay accountable and motivated.

Ultimately, the key is to stop being a passive spectator in our own lives and to start taking an active role in our growth and transformation. As the Apostle Paul wrote, *"Whatever you do, work at it with all your heart, as working for the Lord, not for human masters."* (Colossians 3:23)

This verse reminds us that the work of personal growth and transformation is not just for our benefit, but for the glory of God. When we take action and put our faith into practice, we open ourselves up to the transformative power of the Holy Spirit, who can work in and through us to bring about the change we desire.

Of course, the journey of taking action and leaving the past behind is not always an easy one. There will be setbacks, obstacles, and moments of doubt and fear. But it's important to remember that growth and change are rarely as easy as ABC or 123; they often involve two steps forward and one step back.

The key is to persevere, to keep moving forward, even when the path ahead seems uncertain. As the Prophet Isaiah reminds us, *"Forget the former things; do not dwell on the past. See, I am doing a new thing! Now it springs up; do you not perceive it? I am making a way in the wilderness and streams in the wasteland."* (Isaiah 43:18-19)

This powerful verse encourages us to let go of the past and to keep our eyes fixed on the new things that God is doing in our lives. Even when the path ahead seems daunting or unclear, we can trust that God is at work, preparing the way and providing the resources and support we need to keep moving forward.

So, let us take courage and step out in faith, trusting in the God who can do *"immeasurably more than all we ask or imagine"* (Ephesians 3:20). Let us be like Noah, taking action in response to God's call, even when the task seems impossible. And let us be like the seed, breaking open and stretching towards the sun, determined to fulfill our God-given potential.

The road ahead may not be easy, but it is the only way to truly leave the past behind and embrace the new life that God has in store for us. So, let us take action, one step at a time, and watch as the transformative power of God unfolds in our lives.

Chapter 11
Embracing the Unknown
The freedom of letting go

We live in a world where we crave certainty and control, the idea of embracing the unknown can seem frightening. We often find ourselves clinging to the familiar, afraid to take a step into the unknown. However, it is precisely in this act of letting go that we can discover a profound sense of freedom and personal growth.

Some time ago, I met a young lady who was in such an uncomfortable situation but was so afraid of the unknown, that she stayed until it started to affect her negatively. Ionie is a young woman who has lived her entire life in the confines of her family home. She had never known the experience of living independently, always relying on the support and security of her family members. However, the conditions in her family home had become increasingly uncomfortable, with limited resources and constant tension. Despite this, Ionie was paralyzed by the fear of the unknown, unable to imagine what it would be like to venture out on her own.

Ionie's situation is not uncommon. Many individuals find themselves trapped in uncomfortable or even unhealthy situations, but the prospect of the unknown holds them back. They cling to the familiar, even if it's draining their resources and depleting their well-being because the alternative seems too risky or overwhelming.

In Ionie's case, the fear of the unknown was heightened by her lack of experience living alone. She had never had to manage her finances, household chores, or daily routines without the safety net of her family. The thought of stepping into this unknown territory was enough to keep her anchored in the past, unable to envision a future where she could thrive independently. She even made a plausible argument, alluding to the economy and how expensive renting a home was.

Truth be told, people are making way less than many of us and they are doing that and more. Moreover, our heavenly father knows what we need, and He is faithful to provide for us. We often stay bound and do not enter the fullness of what God has for us, never stepping into our land of milk and honey. We must refuse every self-imposed limitation because clinging to the past is very costly.

Ionie's resources were dwindling, and the emotional toll of the uncomfortable living situation was taking a significant toll on her mental health. She knew deep down that something had to change, but the fear of the unknown held her back.

This reluctance to let go is not limited to living situations. It can also manifest in our relationships. Many people find themselves trapped in unhealthy or unfulfilling relationships, whether it's a toxic friendship, a stagnant romantic partnership, or an extra-marital affair. They cling to these connections because they provide a sense of familiarity and security, even if the relationship is ultimately draining and preventing them from finding true fulfillment.

I have watched people close to me stay in relationships that had become so taxing, and abusive just because children were involved. I'd often hear them saying "I am doing this for the kids" or "How will I manage on my own with two or three kids", enduring the abusive cycle repeatedly. Having experienced this firsthand, let me just say, that you serve your children when you serve yourself. You can only love your children to the extent to which you love yourself.

Having a child constantly hearing the cursing, seeing the fights, and then experiencing the emotional leakage only breaks down that child. Especially when we know that you want to leave and you are staying for us, it leaves us with a sense of guilt, it is very painful, when we come home to a place that should be our shelter, and day after day, we experience World War III and IV more than peace, love and joy.

Abuse comes in many forms and while the other parent may be the one experiencing physical blows, the child is experiencing said abuse. This abuse may be experienced more on an emotional level. A physical blow may cool down, but the damage done emotionally may be left for years. We find when children experience these things they act out in schools, become unrelatable, and often hurt themselves and others. When we have consistently seen those, we love being broken piece by piece, losing a little piece of ourselves every day all in the name of 'love or wanting the best for my children', my dear is not love that's sacrifice in every sense of the word. I know you must make sacrifices for your children, and

I would never dispute that but not that kind of sacrifice that jeopardizes your health and mental space.

These are the very things that keep us anchored in the past and we find that we spend a great amount of our adult life unlearning these things and dealing with the trauma they imposed, not to mention it give us a false sense of what love is. A nuclear family is ideal, we all want to grow up with both parents. We would rather enjoy both parents separately in a safe, loving, and welcoming environment. So, if you are battling with a similar situation, pray about it and remember that co-parenting is always an option.

The truth is the only constant in life is change. By clinging to the known, we often miss out on the endless possibilities that lie ahead. When we let go of the need to control every aspect of our lives, we open ourselves up to new experiences, perspectives, and paths that may be infinitely more fulfilling than the ones we had previously envisioned.

In the case of an extra-marital affair, for example, an individual may stay involved simply because they know that person is always there for them, even on their lowest days. They may be reluctant to let go of this familiar presence, even if the affair is preventing them from fully committing to a more promising relationship. The fear of the unknown – of what it would be like to be without that familiar support – can be a powerful deterrent to letting go. A full hand cannot take a gift basket without first putting down what's in said hands. Let go of what belongs to someone else so that you can receive your package.

This reluctance to let go often stems from a deeper fear of being hurt. We hold on to what we know, even if it's not serving us because we're afraid of the pain and uncertainty that can come with the unknown. We'd rather cling to the familiar, even if it's depleting us than risk the vulnerability of opening ourselves up to something new.

However, this mentality can ultimately hold us back from experiencing true freedom and personal growth. When we cling to the past or try to control every aspect of our lives, we often end up feeling stuck and anxious, unable to embrace the wonders that the unknown may hold.

It is in the act of letting go that we can truly open ourselves up to the possibilities that lie ahead. By releasing our grip on the familiar, we create space for something new and potentially more fulfilling to enter our lives. This doesn't mean abandoning all planning or decision-making – it's about finding a balance between having a vision for the future and being open to the unexpected.

For Ionie, the decision to let go and venture out on her own was a difficult one, but it ultimately proved to be a liberating experience. She took the leap, moved out of her family home, and began to explore the world on her terms. At first, it was overwhelming and uncertain, but gradually, she began to discover a newfound sense of independence and self-reliance.

As she navigated the challenges of living alone, Ionie learned valuable skills and gained a deeper understanding of herself. She discovered passions and interests that she had never explored before, and she began to cultivate a sense of purpose and direction in her life. The fear of the unknown gradually gave way to a sense of excitement and possibility.

Similarly, in the realm of personal relationships, letting go can be a powerful act of liberation. When we're willing to release our grip on unhealthy or unfulfilling connections, we create space for more meaningful and fulfilling relationships to emerge. This doesn't mean that the process is easy – it often involves facing the pain and vulnerability of letting go. But by doing so, we can prevent ourselves from staying anchored in the past and instead focus on building a future that aligns with our values and desires.

The story of Joseph in the Book of Genesis provides a powerful example of the transformative power of embracing the unknown. After being betrayed and sold into slavery by his brothers, Joseph could have clung tightly to the trauma of his past, allowing resentment and bitterness to define the trajectory of his life. Instead, he chose to let go, to surrender himself to the uncertainty of his new circumstances, and to trust in the unfolding of a greater plan.

As Joseph navigated the challenges of slavery and eventual imprisonment, he demonstrated unwavering resilience and adaptability. He did not waste his energy fighting against the hand he had been dealt, but rather, he focused his efforts on making the most of each present moment. By embracing the unknown, Joseph discovered hidden reservoirs of strength and wisdom within himself, qualities that would eventually propel him to a position of great leadership and influence.

So often in life, we cling tightly to the familiar. We cling tightly to the trauma of his past, allowing resentment and bitterness to take us over, using the hand we've been dealt as a crutch. We justify why we are where we are, using the many injustices as crutches but like Joseph, we must break free as those excuses are keeping us anchored in the past.

The truth is we are born looking like our families, but we die looking like our experiences and our choices. We must decide every day that we are going to make the most of every moment. What are you using as your crutch?

I watched my mother for years, holding on to the fact that she got pregnant in high school using that as an excuse for why she was where she was. Now more than ever not completing high school is no longer an excuse, there are so many schools now that cater to persons who cannot read to those who didn't finish their high school education. The Bible says in Genesis

27:40, "...but when you become restless, you shall break the yoke from your neck".

I watched my mother rise like a phoenix from the ashes, go back to school, pursue her passion, and is now a Japanese Chef. Had she continued to dance to the hook of the song of what happened to her she would have still been living in a chapter that no longer served her. You too, can exit that narrative that keeps you anchored.

If you want to return to school, go for it. Don't let the fear of being "too old" or the concern that you may not know what to do hold you back. The unknown can be intimidating, but it is also where the potential for profound transformation lies. By embracing uncertainty and taking the leap, you individual may discover a newfound passion, acquire invaluable knowledge and skills, and inspire others who are wrestling with similar fears.

The freedom that comes with embracing the unknown is not always easy to attain, but it is undoubtedly worth the effort. When we let go of the limiting beliefs and preconceptions that have been holding us back, we unlock a world of possibilities. We become open to new perspectives, unexpected opportunities, and the chance to reinvent ourselves in ways that align with our deepest aspirations.

I have observed that, many of us especially born-again believers; we embrace 1 Corinthians 15:22, claiming the life we now have through Christ Jesus. We believe that the sin that entered the world through Adam's disobedience no longer defines us but rather, the redemption and freedom that Christ has secured for us. We claim that for our spiritual walk but refuse to embrace this truth in the physical aspects of our day-to-day lives.

We hold so tightly to our mistakes and the struggles we encountered, using them as crutches as to why we remain where we are, refusing to go beyond them. We cling to the pain, shame, and bondages of our yesterday even though God has promised to make all things new. Step out, refuse to use the things that happened or are happening to us as justification for lack of progress, and embrace freedom, as that is the only way to truly live a victorious life.

I understand that the routines, relationships, and possessions that have defined us for years or even decades provide a sense of security. They provide a sense of security; a foundation we can rely on amidst the chaos of an unpredictable world. But this comfort comes at a price. When we refuse to let go of the past, we stifle our growth and development. We deny ourselves the opportunity to evolve, to reinvent who we are, and to explore the vast unknown that lies beyond our self-imposed boundaries.

When we embrace the unknown, we open ourselves up to limitless possibilities. The future is a blank canvas, waiting to be filled with our dreams, our passions, and our most authentic selves. By letting go of the anchors that have held us back, we can set sail towards uncharted waters, discovering new landscapes within ourselves and in the world around us.

In a world that craves certainty and predictability, the notion of embracing the unknown can be both exciting and frightening. However, it is often in the unfamiliar that we find the greatest opportunities for growth, self-discovery, and personal transformation.

This journey is not without its challenges. The unknown can be terrifying, filled with uncertainty and the risk of failure. But it is also where the greatest growth and transformation occur. It is where we shed the old to make way for the new, shedding layers of conditioning, fear, and self-doubt to reveal the truest expression of who we are.

Like Joseph, we may be called to step into the unknown amid great adversity and pain. But it is in these moments of darkness that the seeds of our greatest growth are sown. By embracing the uncertainty of the present, we can let go of the anchors of the past and allow ourselves to be carried by the tides of change, trusting that we will ultimately arrive at a destination more fulfilling and purposeful than we ever could have imagined.

So let us take inspiration from Joseph's journey and summon the courage to loosen our grip on the familiar.

For in the freedom of the unknown, we will find the freedom to become the truest expressions of ourselves - unbound by the limitations of our past and empowered to create a future that aligns with our deepest values and aspirations.

In the end, the freedom of letting go is not about abandoning the past, but about integrating it into a new vision for the future. It is about honouring the lessons we have learned, the relationships that have shaped us, and the experiences that have made us who we are. But it is also about recognizing that the past does not have to define us and that the true path to growth and fulfillment lies in our willingness to embrace the unknown.

In the face of change and the unknown, it is natural to feel a sense of nervousness. But as we cultivate a mindset of curiosity, courage, and resilience, we can learn to see the unknown as a canvas upon which we can paint the masterpiece of our lives. By stepping out of our comfort zones and embracing the boundless potential that lies ahead, we can unlock a level of freedom and fulfillment that was previously unimaginable.

So let us set sail into the vast expanse of possibility, trusting in the currents of change and the wisdom of the unknown. It is only by letting go that we can truly become anchored in the present, embracing the freedom to create the life we have always imagined.

Chapter 12
Rewriting The Narrative
Forging The Path Forward

It is often said that the journey of life is not a straight and narrow path, but rather a winding road filled with unexpected twists and turns. This was the case for me, as I navigated the transition from high school to university.

In high school, I had been the "bright spark" and "head girl," known for my academic ability and consistently achieving high marks, often reaching the coveted "A" grade. I was the first person in your family to venture into the realm of higher education, a milestone that filled me with great excitement.

However, as I stepped onto the university campus, the challenges I faced quickly became apparent. Unlike the structured environment of high school, where I had thrived, the university presented a new set of obstacles. The lack of financial resources and the absence of familial guidance made the journey particularly overwhelming.

To make ends meet, I found myself working a full-time job, clocking in at 8 am and not returning home until 10 pm. The commute, which involved navigating two modes of transportation, added an hour and a half to my daily schedule. As a 17-year-old, I was not mentally or emotionally prepared for this grueling routine.

The strain of balancing work, classes, and the demands of university life took a toll, and I found myself struggling academically. The "bright spark" I had been in high school seemed to dim as I failed three modules in my first year. This was a devastating blow to my self-confidence, and I began to question my abilities and worth.

In the face of this overwhelming setback, it would have been understandable to succumb to the narrative of failure. But I chose a different path. Though I retreated from social circles, feeling like a failure and stuck in a cycle of self-doubt, I refused to let that be the end of my story.

Ten years later, my journey has taken an inspiring turn. Not only have I graduated from university but have also built a successful career and even started my own business. This remarkable transformation is a testament to my unwavering determination and my ability to rewrite the narrative of my life.

I have discovered, the process of rewriting the narrative is not an easy one. It requires a conscious effort to shift your mindset, embrace the struggle as an opportunity for growth, and trust in the redeeming power of God.

In the scriptures, we find encouragement and guidance for those who find themselves in similar situations. The Apostle Paul reminds us, "And we know that in all things God works for the good of those who love him, who have been called according to his purpose" (Romans 8:28). This promise of God's divine intervention and the assurance that He can use our struggles for our ultimate good is a powerful foundation upon which to build our lives.

For those who are currently rewriting their narratives, here are some steps you can take to forge a path forward:

1. Acknowledge and Embrace the Struggle

-Recognize that your current situation is not a reflection of your worth or your abilities. It is simply a phase in your journey, a challenge to be overcome.

-Embrace the struggle as an opportunity for growth and transformation. As the saying goes, "The darkest night is often the bridge to the brightest day."

2. Renew Your Mindset

-Shift your perspective from one of defeat to one of resilience. Remind yourself that you have the power to rewrite your story.

-Affirmations can be a powerful tool in rewiring your brain. Speak words of encouragement and believe in your ability to overcome.

-Surround yourself with positive influences, whether it's inspirational books, podcasts, or the company of those who uplift and encourage you.

3. Seek Support and Community

-Reach out to your support system, whether it's family, friends, or a faith community. Isolation can only make the journey harder.

-Engage with the fellowship of believers, as the Bible instructs us not to neglect "the assembling of ourselves together" (Hebrews 10:25). The church is a haven of support and encouragement.

-Be vulnerable and share your struggles. You may be surprised by the empathy and guidance you receive.

4. Develop a Practical Plan

-Break down your goals into manageable steps. Create a roadmap that outlines the specific actions you need to take.

-Prioritize self-care and balance. Ensure that you are taking care of your physical, mental, and emotional well-being.

-Seek professional guidance if needed, whether it's academic counseling, financial advice, or mental health support.

5. Embrace the Lessons and Grow

-Reflect on the lessons you have learned from your struggles. How have they shaped and refined you?

-Recognize that the challenges you have faced are not wasted; they are stepping stones to your transformation.

-Commit to using your experiences to empower and inspire others who may be walking a similar path.

Remember, your story is not defined by your past failures or struggles; it is defined by your resilience, your courage, and your willingness to forge a new path. Embrace the journey, trust in God's timing, and keep moving forward, one step at a time. The future that lies ahead is brighter than you can imagine.

As we approach the end of our transformative journey, we find ourselves standing at a crossroads - the past receding in the distance, the future stretching out before us, brimming with possibility. It is here, in this pivotal moment, that we are called to make a choice: will we continue to be bound by the narratives of our past, or will we summon the courage to rewrite the scripts that have defined us?

The story of the Apostle Paul provides a powerful testament to the transformative power of rewriting one's narrative. Once a zealous persecutor of

Christians, Paul encountered the risen Christ on the road to Damascus, an event that dramatically altered the course of his life (Acts 9:1-19). In that moment, Paul was forced to confront the flaws in the narrative he had constructed for himself - one of religious zeal and moral superiority.

But rather than cling to the past, Paul embraced the unknown, allowing his encounter with Jesus to rewrite the very foundation of who he was.

Similarly, Jesus himself embodied the freedom of letting go and forging a new path forward. Throughout his ministry, he challenged the rigid religious narratives of his day, offering a radical vision of a Kingdom built on love, mercy, and grace. Rather than be confined by the expectations of others, Jesus boldly rewrote the script, choosing to walk a path that was often lonely and misunderstood, but ultimately transformative for all who encountered him.

Like Paul and Jesus, we too are called to the courageous act of rewriting our narratives. For too long, many of us have been slaves to the stories we've told ourselves - the limiting beliefs, the negative self-talk, the predetermined notions of who we are and what we're capable of achieving. These narratives, forged in the crucible of our life experiences, have become the shackles that confine us, robbing us of the freedom to truly become the authors of our own lives.

But the time has come to break free. To pick up the pen and rewrite the script, sculpting a new vision for our future that is unbound by the constraints of what has come before. This is no easy task - it requires us to face our deepest fears, challenge the deeply held beliefs that have shaped our worldview, and confront the parts of ourselves we've been too afraid to acknowledge.

Yet, in doing so, we unleash a truly transformative power. By taking control of our narrative, we reclaim our agency, our autonomy, and our capacity to shape the trajectory of our lives. We can shed the skin of our former selves, shedding the roles and identities that no longer serve us, and step into the fullness of who we are meant to become.

And here, during this profound transformation, we find the hope and possibility that our faith in Jesus Christ promises. For just as Paul was redeemed and transformed by his encounter with the living Christ, so too can we be empowered to rewrite the narratives that have constrained us. Through the grace, love, and redemption offered by our Savior, we are freed from the weight of our past and given the courage to forge a new path forward

This process of rewriting our narrative is not a one-time event, but an ongoing practice of self-reflection, self-discovery, and self-expression. It means continually examining the stories we tell ourselves, questioning the assumptions that underlie them, and having the courage to revise them as we grow and evolve.

It means cultivating a mindset of curiosity and wonder, approaching each new chapter of our lives with a beginner's mind. It means letting go of the need to have all the answers, and instead, embracing the uncertainty of the journey ahead.

And as we do this work, we open ourselves up to a world of infinite possibility. The shackles of the past begin to fall away, and we find ourselves standing on the precipice of a future that is ours to shape. We can dream bigger, take bolder risks, and chase the passions that ignite our souls, secure in the knowledge that our Savior walks beside us, guiding and empowering us every step of the way.

In this final chapter, we celebrate the transformative power of rewriting our narratives. We honour the courage it takes to shed the skin of the old, to leave behind the things that no longer serve us, and to forge a new path forward. We embrace the freedom that comes from becoming the authors of our own lives, unbound by the limitations of the past and empowered to create a future that aligns with our deepest values and aspirations.

So let us pick up our pens, our paintbrushes, our instruments of self-expression, and begin to weave a new tapestry of our lives. Let us rewrite the stories that have confined us, and unleash the full force of our creativity, our resilience, and our unwavering belief in our potential. In doing so, we will not only transform our own lives but inspire others to do the same - creating a ripple effect of change that can reshape the very fabric of our world.

Throughout your journey, remember the words of the Apostle Paul: "And we know that in all things God works for the good of those who love him, who have been called according to his purpose" (Romans 8:28). Trust in God's plan for your life, even when the path ahead seems unclear.

As you continue to rewrite your narrative, may you find strength in the knowledge that you are not alone.

The church and the fellowship of believers are there to support and encourage you. Lean on your faith, your community, and your determination, and know that you are capable of overcoming any obstacle that stands in your way.

The road ahead may be uncertain, but it is also filled with boundless possibilities. Let us approach it with open hearts, curious minds, and the unwavering conviction that we have the power to forge a new path forward - one that honors our past, embraces the present, and propels us toward a future that is entirely our own, empowered by the transformative grace of our Lord and Savior, Jesus Christ.

Conclusion

As the final pages of this book come to a close, it's clear that the journey of embracing the unknown and leaving behind the past has been a challenging, yet transformative one. I hope that you were motivated by the ideas presented within these chapters and I encourage you to rethink your relationship with the past and consider how it is shaping your present and future.

Throughout this exploration, we've delved into the complex emotions and thought patterns that often keep us tethered to the familiar, even when it no longer serves us. The temptation to cling to the past, whether it be through unhealthy habits, toxic relationships, or a refusal to adapt to change, is a deeply human experience. But as we've discovered, true freedom and growth can only be found in our willingness to let go and step into the unknown.

One of the central themes that has emerged is the idea that the past does not have to define us. While it is natural and even important to reflect on our experiences and learn from them, we do not have to be held captive by them. The past is a part of our story, but it does not have to be the entire narrative. By embracing this mindset, we open ourselves up to the possibility of transformation and the opportunity to write a new chapter that aligns with our deepest values and aspirations.

As we consider the road ahead, it's clear that the path forward is not always clear-cut or easy to navigate. The unknown can be daunting, filled with uncertainty and the potential for both triumph and setback. But it is precisely in these moments of vulnerability and discomfort that we find the greatest potential for growth and self-discovery.

This is where the true power of faith comes into play. For those who believe in Jesus Christ, the path to true liberation from the past and embrace of the unknown is not a solitary one. Through a relationship with our Savior, we are granted the strength, wisdom, and guidance to face the challenges that lie ahead. His word assures us that *"all who call on the name of the Lord will be saved"* (Romans 10:13), and it is this promise that can anchor us in the face of the unknown.

It is important to note that the decision to accept Jesus Christ as our Lord and Savior is not one to be taken lightly. It requires a deep and sincere commitment to surrendering our lives to His will and trusting in His plan for our lives. But for those who take this step, the rewards are immeasurable. Through the power of the Holy Spirit, we are empowered to let go of the past, embrace the unknown, and walk in the freedom that can only be found in a life lived for Christ.

As we reflect on the journey that has brought us to this point, it is essential to remember that the work of transformation is ongoing. There will be moments of triumph and moments of struggle, but it is in these moments that we can find the strength to press on, knowing that we are not alone. With Jesus Christ as our anchor, we can face the unknown with confidence and hope that transcends our limited understanding.

In the end, the conclusion of this book is not a definitive end, but rather a starting point for a new and exciting chapter. By embracing the unknown and leaving behind the things that no longer serve us, we open ourselves up to a world of possibilities – a world where we can grow, thrive, and become the best versions of ourselves. And with Jesus Christ as our guide, we can be assured that the path ahead, though not without its challenges, will be one of purpose, meaning, and eternal hope.

So, let us take this final step with courage, faith, and a renewed sense of purpose. Let us leave behind the shackles of the past and step boldly into the unknown, trusting in the love and grace of our Savior to lead us to the fulfillment of His perfect plan. For it is in this surrender that we will find the true liberation and freedom that our hearts have been longing for all along.

Salvation Prayer

Have you ever made Jesus the Lord and Savior of your life?

If not, pray this prayer and start a new life in Christ.

Dear God,

I come to You in the Name of Jesus. I admit that I am not right with You, and I want to be right with You. I ask You to forgive me of all my sins. The Bible says if I confess with my mouth that "Jesus is Lord," and believe in my heart that God raised Him from the dead, I will be saved (Rom. 10:9). I believe with my heart, and I

*confess with my mouth that Jesus
is the Lord and Savior of my life.
Thank You for saving me!*

In Jesus' Name, I pray. Amen.

Get into a bible-based church and remain anchored in Christ for His anchor holds amidst the storms. Let him hold your hands as you embrace change and leave behind the places that no longer serve you.

About the Author

Shanique Bruce is a dedicated mom and wife. She is a graduate of the University of Technology Jamaica. She is the C.E.O of candledbyshan and she also serves in the healthcare sector. Shanique, now author and coach, is passionate about helping others overcome the challenges of their pasts.

As a survivor herself, she uses her own experiences to inspire and guide people toward personal transformation.

Driven by her strong Christian faith, Shanique is dedicated to supporting individuals in breaking free from the anchors of the past so they can embrace a brighter future.

Made in the USA
Middletown, DE
26 November 2024